DORIAN

Phoebe Eclair-Powell and Owen Horsley
Adapted from *The Picture of Dorian Gray* by Oscar Wilde

The first performance of *DORIAN*
was at Reading Rep Theatre
on 13 October 2021

DORIAN

Phoebe Eclair-Powell and Owen Horsley

Actor 1	Andro Cowperthwaite (He/Him/They)
Actor 2	Nat Kennedy (They/Them)
Actor 3	Ché Francis (They/Them)
Director	Owen Horsley (He/Him)
Designer	E.M. Parry (They/Them)
Lighting Designer	Simeon Miller (He/Him)
Sound Designer	Jasmin Kent Rodgman (She/Her)
Movement Director	Kloé Dean (She/Her)
Casting Director	Annelie Powell CDG (She/Her)
Costume Supervisor	Fran Levin (They/Them)
Assistant Director	Annie Kershaw (She/Her)
Associate Lighting Designer	Adam Jeffreys (He/Him)
Stage Manager	Eleanor Walton
Production Manager	Jordan Harris (He/Him)
Production Assistant	Jamie Kubisch-Wiles (He/Him)
DORIAN artwork design	Muse Creative Communications

Andro Cowperthwaite (Actor 1) (He/Him/They)

Andro is an actor and singer/songwriter and trained at Drama Centre London. Andro's self produced and written debut EP *MORTAL* was released in July 2021. His theatre credits include *The Lion, The Witch and The Wardrobe* (Bridge Theatre); *Salome and Dido: Queen of Carthage* (RSC) and *Corpus Christi* (The Space). His film credits include *Cold Blow Lane*, *The Agency*, *Abstract* and *PREY* (BFI).

Nat Kennedy (Actor 2) (They/Them)

Nat is a recent RADA graduate and queer theatre and filmmaker. They co-founded The Sirrah Sisters, a female and non-binary Shakespeare Theatre Company. Their previous credits include *The Maids* (Southwark Playhouse); *Iphigenia in Aulis* (The Cockpit Theatre); *A Midsummer Night's Dream* and *Twelfth Night* (The Sirrah Sisters); and *Macbeth*, *As You Like It* and *Henry V* (The Show Must Go Online).

Ché Francis (Actor 3) (They/Them)

Ché is a recent LAMDA graduate, and their theatre credits include *Curtain Up* and *The Assassination of Katie Hopkins* (Theatr Clwyd); *Love, Childhood & War* (National Theatre); *The Colours* (Soho Theatre); *Volpone* (Omnibus Theatre) and *The Toxic Avenger* (Arts Theatre West End). Film and TV credits include *Nectarine* (BBC) and *Medea* (BFI).

Phoebe Eclair-Powell (Writer) (She/Her)

Phoebe is the current winner of the Bruntwood Prize for her play *Shed: Exploded View*. Past theatre credits include *Harm* (Bush Theatre); *Really Big and Really Loud* (Paines Plough Roundabout); *The Picture of Dorian Gray* (Watermill), *These Bridges* (NT Connections) *Fury* (Soho Theatre); *TORCH* (pleasance); *Epic Love and Pop Songs* (Pleasance); *WINK* (Theatre503). Her TV credits include: *Harm* (BBC); *Two Weeks to Live* (Sky); and *Hollyoaks* (Channel 4).

Owen Horsley (Writer and Director) (He/Him)

Owen's theatre credits include *Maydays, Salome, The Famous Victories of Henry V, Henry VI Part 1: Open Rehearsal Project* (co-directed with Gregory Doran) (Royal Shakespeare Company); *Hamlet* (CSC, New York); *Don Giovanni* (LaMaMa, New York); *A Midsummer Night's Dream* (Garsington Opera); *Henry V* (Shanghai Dramatic Arts Centre); *The Picture of Dorian Gray* (Watermill Theatre); *The Richard Project*

(American Academy); *Outside on the Street* (Arcola Theatre/Edinburgh Festival); *Edward II* (St Andrew's Crypt). Owen created Bard City in 2016, offering Shakespeare training in New York and London as well as presenting innovative versions of his plays. He is an Associate Director for Cheek By Jowl.

E.M. Parry (Designer) (They/Them)

Mallin is a designer and visual artist working across theatre, opera, Queer cabaret and drag, specialising in work which centres Queer bodies and narratives. They are an Associate Artist of Shakespeare's Globe, a previous winner of the Jocelyn Herbert Award for Scenography, and a Linbury Prize finalist. Theatre includes *Hamlet*, *As You Like It* (Shakespeare's Globe); *Translyria* (Sogn go Fjordane Teater, Norway); *Effigies of Wickedness* (Gate Theatre/ENO); *Rotterdam* (UK Tour/Arts Theatre/59E59/Trafalgar Studios 2/Theatre503. Olivier Award for Outstanding Achievement in an Affiliate Theatre); *We Dig* (Emma Frankland & Co./Oval House); *Grimm Tales* (Unicorn Theatre); *The Strange Undoing of Prudencia Hart* (New Vic Theatre); *Here I Belong*, *Milked*, *Each Slow Dusk* (Pentabus); *Posh* (Nottingham Playhouse/Salisbury Playhouse); *The Miser* (Watermill Theatre) and others. Their designs were recently included in Staging Places: UK Design for Performance (V&A Museum). Mallin trained at Motley and Wimbledon School of Art.

Simeon Miller (Lighting Designer) (He/Him)

Simeon graduated from Mountview Academy in 2010 and has since worked as a Lighting Designer, based in London. He works across theatre, dance, musicals, 'gig theatre' and devised work. He enjoys contributing to new writing, especially socially and politically conscious work which amplifies oppressed and radical voices. Recent credits include *Notes on Grief* (MIF); *Black Holes* (UK Tour); *Subject Mater* (Edinburgh Fringe); *The Mob Reformers* (Lyric Hammersmith); *High Rise State of Mind* (UK Tour); *Do You Love This Planet* (Tristan Bates Theatre); *The Art of Gaman* (Theatre503).

Jasmin Kent Rodgman (Sound Designer) (She/Her)

British-Malaysian Composer & Sound Designer Jasmin Kent Rodgman brings together the contemporary classical, electronic and sound design worlds to create powerful soundscapes and musical identities. Working across theatre, film and the concert hall, her work has most recently been featured on BBC Radio 3, BBC Four, BBC Arts, at Theatr Clwyd and the Bush Theatre, and at Sundance and SXSW Film Festivals. She is a previous British Council & PRS Musician in Residence: China and London Symphony Orchestra Jerwood Composer. Often collaborating with other artforms to produce her own interdisciplinary projects, her work has been performed across the UK and internationally with partners such as London Fashion Week, World Music Festival Shanghai, Edinburgh International Festival, Wilderness Festival, the Roundhouse, Shoreditch Town Hall, Barbican, Oxford Playhouse and the Royal Albert Hall.

Kloé Dean (Movement Director) (She/Her)

Kloé Dean is a Choreographer, Movement Director and Performing Artist from London, UK. Specialising in Hip Hop, Funk and Streetdance Styles. With an array of knowledge, experience, expertise and skillsets spanning close to twenty years, she draws from these styles to create, perform and facilitate across Theatre, TV, Film, Music, Fashion, Corporate, Community and Education. Kloé has worked with a range of Music artists such as Little Mix, Little Simz, Cleo Sol and Rita Ora. Brands such as Nike, George at ASDA and Marks & Spencer's. Kloé has developed movement for a range of theatre works most recently working on Paines Plough's Roundabout Season of four new plays touring the UK. Alongside dance theatre presented both nationally and internationally including platforms such as Breakin Convention in London, Ladies Of Hip Hop in New York and Sub-Urban Danse Festival Copenhagen.

Annelie Powell CDG (Casting Director) (She/Her)

Annelie Powell CDG is a Casting Director for theatre, television and film, working prolifically across a variety of theatres on a freelance basis. Recent credits include: *What's New Pussycat?* (Birmingham Repertory Theatre); *Wendy and Peter Pan* (Leeds Playhouse); *Harm* (Bush Theatre); *The House of Shades* (Almeida Theatre) and *Romeo & Juliet* (Regent's Park). Annelie was previously Head of Casting at Nuffield Theatres for three years and worked at the RSC for five years prior. Her screen work spans projects for Netflix, Apple, Warner Bros, BBC and Nickelodeon amongst others.

Fran Levin (Costume Supervisor) (They/Them)

Fran trained in Costume Design and Realisation at Brighton MET.

Their recent costume credits include costume supervisor for *Let the Right One In* and *Nora* for LAMDA, costume designer for *The Pirate Queen* (The Coliseum); costume designer for *Cats on Stage* (Cyprus) and costume supervisor for Clonter Opera's production of *Don Giovanni*. Fran's other wardrobe credits include 2019 UK Tour of *We Will Rock You*; *Zoonation: Tales of the Turntable* (Southbank Centre); *Man of La Mancha* (The Coliseum); English National Opera 2018-19, *Chicago the Musical* (Phoenix Theatre); *Hair 50th Anniversary Production* (The Vaults). Outside of working in costume, Fran is also a Drag King and violinist.

Annie Kershaw (Assistant Director) (She/Her)

Annie Kershaw is a theatre director and producer. She is a co-founder of Reading-based queer theatre company A Girl Called Stephen Theatre. Directing credits include *Safe* (Reading Rep); *Gigi Star and Her Vocal Cords of Magic* (Applecart Arts); *This Is Not a Protest* (Reading Thames Festival). Her work has been performed at the Lyric, Hammersmith; Pleasance, London; South Street Arts Centre, Reading. Assistant Director credits include *Henry II* (Rabble Theatre); *Alby the Penguin Saves Christmas* (Reading Rep). Annie studied Drama and Theatre Arts at the University of Birmingham.

Adam Jeffreys (Associate Lighting Designer) (He/Him)

Adam is an actor and lighting designer, training at East 15 Acting School and Royal Central School of Speech and Drama. As a production lighting technician, his credits include *The Billy Joel Songbook* (London, 2016/2019); *Peter Pan* (Harlow Playhouse, 2017); *Aladdin* (Harlow Playhouse, 2018); *The Great Christmas Sleigh Ride* (Harlow Playhouse, 2018); *LiveBusiness Entertainment* (Corfu 2018); *Forum Theatre and Education* (Tour of Spain, 2019) and *Wireless Operator* (UK Tour, 2020). Adam is thrilled to be making his Professional Lighting Design debut as an associate with Simeon Miller.

Eleanor Walton (Stage Manager)

Eleanor trained at the Royal Welsh College of Music and Drama. Her theatre credits include *Hound of the Baskervilles* (The Watermill Theatre rural tour); *Belleraphon* (a Boxford Masques production); *You Can't Stop The Beat* (Musical Youth Company of Oxford production). Training credits include *After Rhinoceros: The Red Pill* directed by

Debbie Hannan; *Arcadia* directed by Hannah Noone; *The Merchant of Venice* directed by Patricia Logue; *The Sicilian Courtesan* directed by Laurence Boswell; *Kasimir and Karoline* (UK Premier) directed by Fumi Gomez; *Hedda Gabler* directed by Chelsea Walker; *The Magic Flute* directed by Martin Constantine; *Candide* directed by Andrew Whyment and *One More Look* directed by Kirk Jameson.

Jordan Harris (Production Manager) (He/Him)

Jordan trained in Theatre Production at Guildford School of Acting as a Stage Manager, quickly altering path to become a Production and Technical Manager. His stage management credits include *Eugenius* directed by Ian Talbot (The Other Palace); *No Sound Ever Dies* directed by Lucy Bradley (Brooklands Museum); *Operation Ouch Live!* directed by Peter Adams (Apollo Theatre); *The Red Lion* directed by Sean Turner (Tour). His Production and Technical Management credits include *The New Normal Festival* (London); *Have We Been Here Before* (Immersive Install); Production Manager for GSA (*Titanic the Musical*, *Richard III*, *Who Cares*, and *Sleepy Hollow the Musical*). Jordan is now Head of Production for Reading Rep Theatre and is looking forward to the exciting season ahead.

Reading Rep was founded by Artistic Director Paul Stacey in 2012. He took a £500 overdraft and invested it into his vision to revitalise Reading's cultural landscape by making and creating the highest quality theatre, with, by and for Reading.

The company moved into the black box theatre at Reading College, producing packed-out plays on a shoestring. Before long, Reading Rep grew to be a beloved home and playground for many of the UK's leading theatre-makers, including Barney Norris, Roy Alexander Weise and Mischief Theatre. Collaborations and co-productions with leading regional and London theatres including Nuffield Southampton Theatres, Arcola Theatre and Oxford Playhouse placed Reading within the heart of the national theatre landscape.

With community at the heart of the artistic vision of the company, Reading Rep created ENGAGE in 2015, our flagship community outreach programme providing access to the arts for Reading's most vulnerable communities. We run a year-round programme of workshops, delivered in partnership with Reading Libraries, Reading Borough Council, the Cultural Education Partnership, the NHS and numerous others, that has reached 15,000 children, young people and adults in the last eighteen months alone.

With critical acclaim and sell-out success, Reading Rep was ready for a new and permanent home. In 2018, just six years after our first production, we began raising funds to convert a former Salvation Army Hall into a 170-seat theatre and cultural hub. After raising £1million throughout the Coronavirus pandemic, the company opened its new venue in 2021 with a bold new artistic season of work.

This season of work starts with *DORIAN*, which explores the events that brought Oscar Wilde to Reading Gaol...

For Reading Rep Theatre

Founding Artistic Director – Paul Stacey (He/Him)
Executive Director – Nick Thompson (He/Him)

Associate Director & Director of ENGAGE – Christie O'Carroll (She/Her)
Head of Development – Megan Turnell (She/Her)
Head of Marketing – Zoe Biles (She/Her)
General Manager – Ellie Gavin (She/Her)
Head of Production – Jordan Harris (He/Him)
Producer – Steph Weller (She/Her)
Finance Manager – Sandra Larkin
Press Lead – Kate Morley PR
Production Assistant – Jamie Kubisch-Wiles (He/Him)
ENGAGE Officer – Jasmine Green (She/Her)

Donors and Supporters

Find out more at

readingrep.com

Instagram – @readingrep

Twitter – @ReadingRep

Facebook – ReadingRep

YouTube – Reading Rep Theatre

DORIAN

Phoebe Eclair-Powell and Owen Horsley

Based on *The Picture of Dorian Gray* by Oscar Wilde

The Story of Dorian
Phoebe Eclair-Powell and Owen Horsley

In 2017 the lovely folks at the Watermill asked Phoebe to adapt *The Picture of Dorian Gray* and Owen to direct it for their schools' tour, the idea being to make something accessible and easy for students who were studying the book. The cast would have to be limited to three actors, with minimal set, lighting and costume. We were excited by the challenge and immediately clicked – we wanted to make something boisterous, comic and irreverent. Our references were *Absolutely Fabulous* and *The Neon Demon* – naturally. And we made just that: a fun, frivolous version which potentially lacked the gothic heart of the novel – and indeed the queer perspective that a work of Oscar Wilde's demands. We always promised ourselves that we would do it again one day and redress some of these glaring omissions...

A few years later, and fate would have it that Paul and Nick – the lovely Artistic Director and Exec Producer of Reading Rep – were opening a brand-new theatre in Reading. They had heard of our *Dorian Gray* and were intrigued. When we explained that we wanted to expand on it, were totally up for our queer, experimental version. What became immediately clear was that the story needed to be co-written this time. We would use the material Phoebe had adapted from the book for the most part, but only Owen could bring the heart and the authenticity. We also realised that this story, the story of Dorian Gray, cannot be told in full without discussing the context of the time in which Wilde was writing, and indeed what the book meant for Wilde. After all, the book was used as evidence against him in his trial for gross indecency.

It became abundantly clear that we needed to tell Oscar's story alongside Dorian's, playing with and exploring the almost spooky parallels of love, loss, truth and disillusion. And also – most notably – punishment and shame. This is a story about

Victorian morality and views on sexuality that still preside and cling today. Reading Rep wanted to have an Oscar Wilde in their season because Oscar, of course, went to jail in Reading – and is an icon in the area, albeit for very problematic and traumatic reasons. It felt only right that we told that story on stage – shining a light on how we have tried to glorify a story that actually has a huge amount of sadness to it. And how that story still touches and resonates today.

As such, we have drawn on real-life records of some of Oscar's trials, as well as a kaleidoscope of titbits from various biographies, letters, documentaries, and the team's own modern queer stories – creating a sort of living history alongside Dorian's downfall. This version exposes the queer undertones of the novel and pays homage to the experience of men during the Victorian era who were subject to a law that kept their truth hidden. It is a tapestry of a play that asks the audience to immerse themselves in an ever-changing queer narrative, and to reassess that which we think we know.

But most importantly we wanted to imbue the text with pride, hope, love and, ultimately, queer joy. We hope that this time we have been able to do just that. We hope Oscar likes it.

Characters
to be played by three people

ONE: NARRATOR, DORIAN, LORD ALFRED DOUGLAS
    (BOSIE), MRS VANE
TWO: NARRATOR, BASIL HALLWARD, JAMES VANE,
    ROBBIE ROSS, CARSON (PROSECUTOR), NURSE
THREE: NARRATOR, HENRY WOTTON, OSCAR WILDE,
    SIBYL VANE, ALAN CAMPBELL

Note on the Text

The play blends time and space. Sometimes the narrators
introduce a new section, but you could always add more 'titles'
if you wanted. Music is paramount. Movement and dancing
when it feels right. Singing encouraged. Camp mandatory.
Queerness, of course.

There should be a constant rhythm. The first half is full-on and
energetic; the second more absorbed, ghostly. But there should
always be joy.

A forward slash (/) indicates an interruption.

Now the tricky and ultimate question about how to stage the
painting – this is up to you. We decided to always place the
painting out in the audience, so that people weren't back acting
towards a Hammer Horror painting. We also banned any
'painting acting'.

Our set designer made a brilliantly massive frame with a fun
distorted mirror upstage for our actors to pose/act in, which did
indeed get messier throughout the show as Dorian's soul
exploded.

*This text went to press before the end of rehearsals and so may
differ slightly from the play as performed.*

Prologue

Our three performers are silhouetted onstage. They look marvellous. Drag ball aesthetic. Category is: 'Posing as a Victorian Sodomite'. They should have microphones.

As they walk the runway, they introduce us to the infamous Preface to The Picture of Dorian Gray. *Loud music.*

ONE. *All art is at once surface and symbol.*

TWO. We are posing as three Victorian gentlemen –

THREE. Henry,

TWO. Basil,

ONE. and Dorian.

ONE. More specifically, we are posing as three Victorian sodomites –

TWO. Robbie,

ONE. Bosie,

THREE. and Oscar.

ONE. *The Picture of Dorian Gray.*

THREE. By Oscar Wilde.

TWO. Published 1890.

TWO. We all know it.

ONE. Or at least you've looked up the Wikipedia synopsis.

THREE. Portrait.

TWO. Attic.

ONE. Decadence.

THREE. Sin.

TWO. Et cetera.

ONE. We've been telling it for years.

Those who read beneath the surface do so at their peril.

THREE. If they knew who he really was, they would tremble.

TWO. Maybe that's why we've been telling it for years.

THREE. Who knows?

ONE. *It is the spectator, and not life, that art really mirrors.*

TWO. That's you.

ONE. You're welcome.

THREE. Or maybe it's the author – after all, Oscar Wilde said himself that –

ONE. Dorian was the person he would most like to be.

TWO. Basil was who he was really.

THREE. And Henry was how the world saw him.

TWO. It would be nice if you liked it – but –

ONE. *Diversity of opinion about a work of art shows that the work is –*

THREE. *new –*

ONE. *complex –*

TWO. *and vital.*

ONE. *When critics disagree –*

THREE. *the artist is in accord with himself.*

TWO. The reviews are in –

ONE. 'Mawkish and nauseous.'

THREE. 'Unclean.'

TWO. 'Effeminate.'

ONE. 'Contaminating.'

THREE. 'Why must Oscar Wilde go grubbing in muck heaps?'

TWO. Five hundred words were removed before its next publication.

ONE. Wilde himself removed anything that might be considered… Well, gay…

ONE. *We can forgive a man for making a useful thing as long as he does not admire it.*

THREE. *The only excuse for making a useless thing –*

TWO. *is that one admires it intensely.*

THREE. Oscar fucking Wilde.

TWO. A martyr.

ONE. A saint.

THREE. A sinner.

ONE. An artist.

TWO. A husband.

THREE. A lover.

ONE. A father.

TWO. A homosexual.

THREE. An alcoholic.

TWO. A genius.

THREE. A prisoner.

TWO. A slur.

THREE. A fucking fridge magnet.

ONE. Scene One.
Drawing room. London. Eighteen-something.
Basil and Henry stand, staring at the portrait of Dorian Gray.

TWO. Oh and before we begin –

THREE. Please remember that –

ONE. *ALL ART IS QUITE USELESS.*

ACT ONE

HENRY. So this is it – Basil.
Your newest painting –

BASIL. Yes.

HENRY. It's your best work, you simply must show it at the
Grosvenor –

BASIL. It can never be shown, Henry... it has too much... too
much –

HENRY. / Lust.

BASIL. / soul in it –

HENRY. Whatever – He's pretty.

BASIL. He's more than that.

HENRY. Yes – he's young – perfectly youthful – where on earth
did you pick him up?

BASIL. A party – he entered the room and I knew... that he
was... special.
He's the grandson of Lord Kelso –

HENRY. Oh that filthy rich sadomasochistic pile of sideburns...
didn't he tragically banish his daughter – shame, I hear she
was stunning.

BASIL. Yes the poor boy was brought up all alone in an attic.

HENRY. Quite right, children should be kept out of sight at all
costs.

BASIL. How are yours?

HENRY. No idea... So tell me – how many times have you had
him... sit for you?

BASIL. I have barely let him leave the studio – he is my muse.

HENRY. I can't wait to meet him –

BASIL. I don't want you to meet him.

HENRY. You don't want me to meet him?
But – he's coming here, isn't he – you said –

BASIL. Please, Henry – Dorian Gray is my best friend. If you
met him you would no doubt spoil him. So I would like you
to leave –

HENRY. What nonsense you talk –

BASIL. Please.

DORIAN. Basil?

HENRY. Too late – You must introduce me now.

DORIAN. Sorry I… I didn't know you had company –

BASIL….Dorian – This is… This is Woots.

DORIAN. Woots?

HENRY. A bit of a nickname from the old Oxford days, know
what I mean. Henry Wotton.
Charmed, enchanted and all that – let me touch your hand,
don't be shy.

DORIAN….I'm Dorian Gray.

HENRY. I know exactly who you are, dear.
And may I say, Basil – the painting is good but the real deal
is even more delicious.

DORIAN. Pardon?

BASIL. Nothing.
He's just drooling over you.
We're jealous you see.
We're old and you're young.

DORIAN. Hardly.
Okay, a few years –

HENRY. Decades.

DORIAN. – younger than you but really what's age?

HENRY. Everything.

BASIL. Woots –

HENRY. Sorry – but he deserves to know exactly what he's got. Or did you want to keep him stupid? Wanted to keep him a little bit dumb and pliable...

BASIL. Woots is a terrible influence – so don't believe a word he says –

HENRY. Why, Basil, you know that you used to believe everything I say...

DORIAN. Do I have to pose for you, Basil?

HENRY. Pose?

BASIL. Yes, you stand here and we –

HENRY. Look at you.
    Like a piece of me–/at.

BASIL. Art...

    DORIAN *poses*.

    Thank you, Dorian...

    HENRY *takes out a cigarette case or cigarillos/cigarettes and proceeds to smoke*.

HENRY. I know you hate the smell, Basil, but I'm having one – Dorian?

DORIAN. No I don't smoke... So... are you really as bad... an influence as Basil says you are?

HENRY. Well there is no such thing as a good influence, Dorian –

DORIAN. What do you mean?

HENRY. Well to influence a person is to give him one's soul – he becomes merely an echo of someone else's voice.
    Now to realise oneself completely – that is the aim of the age.

DORIAN. I... I don't get it.

BASIL. You don't have to, he's being / silly –

HENRY. Of course you do – you know exactly what I'm talking
about you just don't want to admit it – let the senses cure the
soul – be the emblem of the age. Show these moral fuckers
what they're missing –
I'm being serious – with your face you could do anything.

DORIAN. You're being ridiculous.

BASIL. See – good boy – chin up.

HENRY. Am I?
Youth is everything, Dorian, don't let anyone tell you
otherwise.
And you possess both youth *and* beauty –

DORIAN. And money – once I turn eighteen –

HENRY. And *that* makes you the most powerful thing on earth
– use it – abuse it –

DORIAN. You're very close all of a sudden.

HENRY. Sorry, just – your skin.
It's radiant.
You know that when you age – all this will be taken from
you – time is a jealous bitch and she will savage a face like
yours, so use it, child – use it whilst you can! Our limbs fail,
our senses rot, we crumble into hideous puppets, we atrophy
until we die, haunted by the exquisite temptations we had not
the courage to yield to.

BASIL. Henry, stop being melodramatic – Dorian, relax –

HENRY. Wouldn't you like to know how powerful you really are?

He offers DORIAN *a toke of his cigarette/cigarillo.*
DORIAN *shakes his head.* HENRY *shrugs it off.*

DORIAN. I do – I think… maybe.

BASIL. Sorry, your expression, it's all wrong – could you
please stop listening, Dorian, I must finish this –

HENRY. Come to the theatre with me tonight, Dorian, come
play with me and my friends –
We'll show you what I mean –

DORIAN. I… I said I'd dine with Basil.

BASIL. Yes he did, Woots – though I may have a bit more work to do on the background.

HENRY. Urgh, how stuffy, how boring, how dullll.

DORIAN. Fine, I'll come, you don't really mind, do you, Basil?

BASIL....Um... not at all.

HENRY. Huzzah!

BASIL. Well at least look at it before you go?

DORIAN *takes a look.*

DORIAN. It's... I am...

HENRY. Beautiful and young and everything.

DORIAN. So sad –

BASIL. Sorry?

DORIAN. I hate it.
It's already younger and more beautiful than I am.
Every second.
Every single second it stays the same, perfect, and I... I will deteriorate and –
Crumble... Atrophy... Rot.
I will die.
And this will remain.
Taunting me –
I would give my very soul to switch places with the face in that portrait.

Some sort of magical crescendo.

BASIL. Don't be silly, child!

DORIAN. Silly? You seem to think everything you disagree with – silly... Lord Henry has taught me something and your painting has proved it – there is nothing but youth, when I grow old I shall simply kill myself!

BASIL. Dorian!
You will always be beautiful to me –

DORIAN. For how long – until the first wrinkle, the first blemish?

HENRY. Fine, if he hates it and you won't exhibit it – I'll buy him – It – the painting.

DORIAN. No! I must have it.

BASIL. It's Dorian's, I promised.

DORIAN. To do what I like with it.

BASIL. As you wish… It was never ever mine.

HENRY. Come along then, dearie – time to play with Uncle Harry.

BASIL. Woots –

HENRY. What?

BASIL. Just remember – what I asked of you –

HENRY. I never keep promises, Basil – not ones I intend to break anyway…

HENRY *exits*.

BASIL *and* DORIAN *alone*.

BASIL. I… I… wish you'd never met him.

DORIAN. It was fate.

BASIL. You said that when you met me.

DORIAN. I have to go –

BASIL. Stay… please –

DORIAN. Have the painting delivered to my house.

BASIL. Dorian –

DORIAN. What?

Pause.

BASIL. I felt something crawl over me… just then – a feeling like…

DORIAN. Goodnight, Basil.

DORIAN *exits*. BASIL *reclines – very Sondheim, very cocktail bar…*

BASIL. How did we meet? The story is simply this... I went to a crush at Lady Brandon's. Well after I had been in the room about ten minutes, I suddenly became conscious that someone was looking at me... I turned halfway around and saw Dorian Gray for the first time... when our eyes met... a curious sensation of terror came over me. I knew then that I had come face to face with someone whose mere personality was so fascinating that if I allowed it to so do it would absorb my whole nature, my whole soul, my very art itself.

BASIL *sings his torch song – 'Always On My Mind' or similar...*

* * *

THREE. Interior – London. 1800. Bosie and Oscar lock eyes across the party...

BOSIE. I'm Alfred, but everyone calls me Bosie.

OSCAR. Then I shall call you Bosie. I'm Oscar, by the way –

BOSIE. I know, you're *the* Oscar Wilde, I read your latest book.

OSCAR. *Dorian Gray*? Did you find it mawkish and nauseous like everyone else?

BOSIE. No – I loved it...

OSCAR. How marvellous.

BOSIE. It was – truly. Everyone at college was desperate to get their hands on my copy – it was perfectly ruined by the time I got it back. I'm at Magdalen by the way.

OSCAR. Oh, the old alma mater – but that's too sad about the copy – here, I have a special version of it – if you like? The unpurged edition...

BOSIE. I'd like that –

OSCAR *and* BOSIE *are pulled towards each other – as he hands over the book.*

ROBBIE. Oscar – there you are – you said we were leaving an hour ago –

OSCAR. Aha, Robbie – Robbie Ross, meet –

BOSIE. Lord Alfred Douglas.

ROBBIE. Sure – Oscar, are you coming or not – we said we would meet these publishers at ten – it's important.

OSCAR. You go ahead –

ROBBIE. Fine.

ROBBIE *leaves*. BOSIE *and* OSCAR *are alone*.

OSCAR. Now where were we – aha, I remember – you were telling me how marvellous my book was –

BOSIE. Yes… I particularly like the way you captured London – the London that we know – the beautiful London.

OSCAR *pulls out a green carnation*.

OSCAR. Do you think this is beautiful?

BOSIE. I do.

OSCAR. You're right. It is sterile. Fabulously sterile. It blossoms purely for joy, for pleasure. It is a work of art. It is beautiful. Just like you, dear boy.

* * *

TWO. The green carnation to which we have referred is a white carnation, dyed by plunging the stem in a dye called malachite green.

ONE. Oscar slipped a green carnation into Bosie's evening coat. Bosie caught himself in the glass. He stood in his favourite stance; left knee bent, arms hanging loosely by his side. Gazing. Gazing like a woman gazes at herself before she starts at a party.

THREE. At the opening night of *Lady Windermere's Fan*, Oscar's bestest best friends – a score of faultless young dandies – scattered themselves in the stalls sporting green carnations.

They all now wear a green carnation.

ONE. Pose.

* * *

*Song: 'Flawless (Go to the City) by George Michael. In the
section below, HENRY and DORIAN cavort, frolic and
vogue across London Town and – indeed – the stage.*

TWO. Henry and Dorian become bestest best 'friends'.

HENRY. Come on, darling boy – it's time to conquer these bona
London streets.

DORIAN. I shouldn't.

HENRY. Couldn't possibly let you leave –

DORIAN. And where are we now –

HENRY. Kettner's, then the Café Royal – Solferino's and a
stiff... drink at the St James's.

DORIAN. I've never been to such places – haven't they um a
reputation.

HENRY. Whatever do you mean? –
Now stir your lallies, you fucking whore.

DORIAN. Should we be in this part of town? I really ought to
go –

HENRY. To the next fucking house party – knock, knock, secret
password –

DORIAN. Are you sure?

HENRY. To the next fucking club!

DORIAN. I suppose this is quite fun, isn't it?

HENRY. Chin up – there's a good boy –

DORIAN. Henry –
I can't feel my face.

HENRY. You've had one too many, dear, now let's have five
more – can't let the dishes clean themselves –

DORIAN. I don't understand what you're saying.

HENRY. You'll soon pick it up. And drink up –

DORIAN. Are you my friend?

HENRY. To the next house and basement and soirée and ball
and vogue vogue vogue.

DORIAN. Everyone's whispering about me, looking at me –

HENRY. You're becoming quite the scenester with that bona ecaf.
I told you I'd make you something more –

DORIAN. More what?

HENRY. Than what you are – a pretty dumb blonde with a huge
cartso – now sniff and line and tag and toke and –

DORIAN. I'm famous now.

HENRY. And rich – Happy birthday by the way.

DORIAN. Stupidly so.
I don't know what to do with my life…

HENRY. This *is* your life.

DORIAN. I can't feel my toes – my martinis are shaking –
Do you remember when you met me?
I shivered.
I knew.
It was fate.
Do you love me?

HENRY. Onwards.

DORIAN. I can't.

HENRY. You can…
Do you know why?

DORIAN. Why?

HENRY. Because you're special.
So much more special than these –
Sad boring ugly shitty mundane, middle-of-the-road,
worthless, ill, boring old losers over there –
Isn't that marvellous, doesn't it just feel glorious?

DORIAN. I can't feel my face… my bona ecaf.
I'm having the best time!
You're my bestest best friend.

HENRY. And Gloria cackled 'Let there be sparkle', and it sparkled.

* * *

TWO. '*The Victorian Homosexual Quiz.*'

THREE. 1800s.

TWO. Were you petted more than most children?

THREE. Is your wrist flat or round?

ONE. Is there much hair on your body?

THREE. Are your shoulders bony or muscular?

TWO. Is there a decided line of femininity to be traced between the base of your neck and the fall of your shoulders?

ONE. Do you whistle well, and naturally like to do so?

TWO. Do you like to play 'coquettishly' with your eyes?

THREE. In grasping anything, as in handshaking and so on, is your grasp vigorous or relatively weak?

TWO. Do you like to dance, and do you take pleasure in athletics?

THREE. Does the theatre deeply interest and affect you?

ALL. GUILTY!

ONE. Everyone was obsessed with Dorian.

THREE. Henry,

TWO. Basil,

ONE. Bosie,

TWO. Robbie,

THREE. Oscar…

ONE. Everyone was obsessed with *us*.

The performers enact Marc-André Raffalovich's 'The World Well Lost', from In Fancy Dress, *1886.*

TWO. Because our world has music,

THREE. and we dance;

TWO. Because our world has colour,

ONE. and They gaze;

TWO. Because our speech is tuned,

THREE. and schooled our glance,

ONE. And we have roseleaf nights and roseleaf days.

THREE. And we have leisure,

TWO. work to do,

ONE. and rest;

THREE. Because They see us laughing when we meet,

TWO. And hear our words and voices,

ONE. see us dressed –
    With skill,

THREE. and pass us and our flowers smell sweet:–

TWO. They think that we know friendship,

ONE. passion,

THREE. love!

TWO. Our peacock, Pride! And Art our nightingale!

THREE. And Pleasure's hand upon our dogskin glove!

TWO. And if they see our faces burn or pale,

THREE. It is the sunlight, think They, or the gas.

ONE. – Our lives are wired like our gardenias.

* * *

OSCAR *applauds as if* BOSIE *has just recited a sonnet.*

OSCAR. Oh, Bosie – huzzah – what poetry you write – it is a
    marvel that those red rose-leaf lips of yours should be made
    no less for the madness of music and song than for the
    madness of kissing.

BOSIE. It's just a little thing.

OSCAR. It is pure passion – you are simply Grecian,
An Olympian,
A god,
A goddess.

BOSIE. You're drunk.

OSCAR. A little.

BOSIE. Ha – I knew it –
I don't want us to leave tomorrow.

OSCAR. Then let's stay – forever.

Silence… unspoken things.

I love you.

BOSIE. You silly old man…

A moment of rejection.

…I love you too.

They go to kiss.

* * *

TWO. We were everywhere.

THREE. The great metropolis of London of which we queers
were the beating heart.

TWO. The railway stations,

ONE. the public baths,

TWO. the arcades,

THREE. the parks,

TWO. the museums and the art galleries,

ONE. the gymnasia,

THREE. the restaurants,

TWO. the public lavatories,

THREE. all of these places formed the perfect environment for
some back-door work.

ONE. And there was another place where we all gathered.

THREE. Where was it now? Oh yeah –

TWO. THE THEATRE.

THREE. Does the theatre deeply interest and affect you?

* * *

ONE. Dorian, now that he's a bit naughty, likes going to playhouses in the rough bit of London Town. Indeed, most nights he goes down a cheap and cheerful music hall and is entranced by this bird called Sibyl who is playing like all the women in Shakespeare –

SIBYL. *O, what a noble mind is here o'erthrown!*
The courtier's, scholar's, soldier's, eye, tongue, sword,
Th'expectancy and rose of the fair state,
The glass of fashion and the mould of form,
Th'observ'd of all observers, quite, quite down!
And I, of ladies most deject and wretched,
That sucked the honey of his music vows,
Now see that noble and most sovereign reason
Like sweet bells jangled out of tune and harsh,
That unmatched form and feature of blown youth
Blasted with ecstasy. O, woe is me,
T'have seen what I have seen, see what I see!

Applause.

DORIAN *goes 'backstage'.* TWO *brings on a clothes rail, etc. When* THREE *has to change from* SIBYL *to* HENRY *to* SIBYL*, they simply go behind the clothes rail and put on their top hat pretending to be at a tailors for a fitting – hiding their skirts, etc.*

DORIAN. I love watching you. You're remarkable. I think your Ophelia is my favourite, but your Juliet and Rosalind are good too and of course your Viola. I have watched you every night.

SIBYL. I know…
    I can see you.

You're the only person who pays for the royal box. That's
why I call you Prince Charming...
Silly... I just don't know your name –

DORIAN. No that's perfect. Call me that – and that's what I
shall be –

SIBYL. I'm Sibyl, Sibyl Vane.

DORIAN. Shhh – you're Ophelia tonight.
This is... this is a madness... but I think we were supposed
to meet –

SIBYL. Fate –

DORIAN. I... I think I love you –

SIBYL. I think I love you too –

TWO. Dorian rushes to tell Henry all about how much he's –

DORIAN. IN LOVE.

HENRY. Cute – now don't ruin it by saying something stupid
like –

DORIAN. I love her.

HENRY. That.

DORIAN. I'm going to propose!

HENRY. Oh Christ –

DORIAN. But I have to – otherwise I can't...

HENRY. Shag her? Are you serious? Dorian, darling, I thought
I'd taught you better than to be so positively Victorian –

DORIAN. Henry! Don't debase the greatest love affair I will
ever have –

HENRY. You're trying too hard – it's really very obvious.

DORIAN. Pardon –

HENRY. Nothing – go on – who is the lucky lucky... *girl*?

DORIAN. Sibyl Vane.

HENRY. Never heard of her –

DORIAN. You soon will – she's just a little actress type thing for now.

HENRY. Oh how amusing.

DORIAN. But I will have her made famous – she's really very talented and very, very poor.

HENRY. Ah, rough trade! She sounds very fashionable indeed.

DORIAN. You're making fun of me.

HENRY. Absolutely –

DORIAN. I wish I had never told you about her –

HENRY. You could not have helped telling me, Dorian, all through your life, you will tell me everything you do…

DORIAN. Well I love her, Henry – I will love her forever –

HENRY. How dull – a woman doesn't make a man, Dorian, she stunts him, I swear I've told you all this before…

DORIAN. I'm going to prove you wrong, Henry – I'll get married and stop hanging out with you and your nasty messed-up friends and listening, always listening to everything you say. When I am with her, I regret everything you have taught me. I grow tired of everything you promised me –

A moment of jealousy…

HENRY. Dear boy, you will never ever, ever grow tired of me – or my friends for that matter.

DORIAN. I'm going to ask her tonight… to marry me.

HENRY. Good luck…

Back to the theatre.

SIBYL. *O, woe is me,*
T'have seen what I have seen, see what I see!

Applause.

DORIAN. Sibyl!

SIBYL. Prince Charming! Did you enjoy it – I never really like playing Ophelia – the bit where she goes mad – and kills herself… it's all so horrid –

DORIAN. You were perfectly charming in death… I want to ask you something – will you… will you marry me? I want you to be all mine – my Juliet, my Hero.

SIBYL. Yes – yes of course I will, Prince Charming –

DORIAN. Kiss me –

SIBYL. I… I… but we're not…

DORIAN. But we are engaged…

SIBYL. Why of course… I just… I…

DORIAN. – Don't you trust me?…

SIBYL. Your face is that of an angel… of course I trust you – I can't wait to be your wife –

They kiss – DORIAN *pushes it – it is implied that they have sex –*

* * *

TWO. Oscar Wilde. Relationship status: married, with children –

ONE. Living in a lovely house in Tite Street, London. Picture perfect.

TWO. Smile.

* * *

THREE. '*The Anatomy of Lying.*'

TWO. There are several reasons why people tell lies:

ONE. To protect themselves from punishment or embarrassment,

THREE. to protect their own fantasies about themselves,

TWO. to protect the feelings – or, in extreme cases, the lives – of others.

THREE. The lies we tell:

TWO. 'I was drunk.'

ONE. 'I'll be away for the weekend.'

TWO. 'I went out with a friend.'

ONE. 'I'm working late.'

THREE. 'I've got a headache.'

ONE. 'It's not who I am.'

TWO. 'I'm going for a walk.'

ONE. The truth is rarely pure –

THREE. and never simple.

> *All very 'happy family' photoshoot, nineties* Hello/OK!
> Magazine.

> *'The Wildes'* Hello *Article.'*

ONE. 16 Tite Street can only be described as an artistic interior with bizarre furnishings, and fabulous ornamentations. Unique in every way.

TWO. The distinguished writer and his wife Constance sit amongst peacock feathers in their luscious drawing room as they discuss their busy lives – juggling theatre success with the pressures of Victorian parenting... I'm equally charmed by their lovely house guest Lord Alfred Douglas Bosie, who stays with the couple now and again.

TWO. They smile and laugh gayly – we are interrupted by yet another friend of the family, a certain Robbie Ross – all three are quite clearly the best of friends – it really is a busy household.

* * *

ONE. Meanwhile.

THREE. On the other side of the river – you know – the poor side with flowing gutters and rats the size of pigs – sits Sibyl Vane – a flower amongst the weeds of her greed-fuelled mother and her dom-top brother.

The next in the style of 1980s EastEnders *– the early days of Pat Butcher meets Victorian melodrama.*

JAMES. What the hell is this marriage thing all about?

MRS V. James, calm yerself!

SIBYL. Mum, did you tell him?!

MRS V. He's got a right ter know – I thought he'd be excited.

JAMES. Excited? – I'm flippin' furious – it ain't happening –

SIBYL. James – don't be like this.

JAMES. I'm about to leave to join the navy, do you really think I'm gunna let you marry some bloke with a posh haircut whilst I'm miles away?

SIBYL. He's a proper gentleman.

JAMES. Yeah, what's his name?

SIBYL. Prince Charming.

JAMES. Cute, you hearing this –

MRS V. He's well fit – anyway I hear he's filthy rich –

JAMES. This is a trap – he's going to shag you and leave you –

SIBYL. It's not a trap… he would never do that…

JAMES. You haven't – have you? You filthy slaaaag.

SIBYL. God no – James, stop it – this is the best thing to have ever happened to me – he's the love of my life.

JAMES. If he turns out to be anything less, if he treats you like anything less – I'll fucking kill him, you hear me?

SIBYL. James –

JAMES. I'll trap him like a rabbit and smash his little skull till his brains spill – you got that?

MRS V. James – leave it out.

JAMES. I won't – not until she says it!

SIBYL. *Fine* – I hear you. Loud and clear.

JAMES. Gunna kiss me goodbye then or what?

MRS V. Ooh, I wonder if he'll buy us a new house –

JAMES. I'm going for a walk –

THREE. Back to the other side of the river – Dorian's side – where the rumour had spread – Dorian Gray, the best bachelor of them all, was to be married on the morn to a worthless penniless actress… shudder…

BASIL. Henry – I'm so confused – is it really true? – that this actress we are watching tonight is the very same person that Dorian intends to marry! It's impossible –

HENRY. Oh I knew ages ago – anyway you better believe it – the boy is simply determined to throw his life away – it's all quite hysterical –

BASIL. Don't you mean awful –

DORIAN. *Woots*, I'm here and ready to get wasted – Oh, Basil, so you decided to come…

BASIL. Yes… so pleased for you…

HENRY. Come on, darling *Dorian*, we are off to my club.

BASIL. Henry – the club!?

HENRY. What? He's ready –

DORIAN. I want to go. Take me –

BASIL. How do you feel about this wedding tomorrow?

HENRY, BASIL *and* DORIAN *stand on the threshold of 'the club'.*

DORIAN. Where are we?

BASIL. Darling, this is Eldorado.

DORIAN. I can hardly see anything.

BASIL. Have you written your vows? You do love Sibyl – don't you?

DORIAN. I want to see her beautiful face next to mine every day, speaking those lines of Shakespeare's greats.

HENRY. Trust me – you feel like that for a year, tops, and then you want to smash it with your fists or smother it with a pillow –

BASIL. Henry!

HENRY. What – fucking honest.

DORIAN. There's no light here?

HENRY. My child, daylight is never admitted here. Such people find life in the artificial light and the incense-laden air, the secret chambers curtained from the hideous glare of the day.

DORIAN. It's strange.

HENRY. Darling, it's bohemian.

BASIL. You shouldn't have brought him.

HENRY. It is his wedding present. Dorian, there is someone I want you to meet –

DORIAN. – what?

BASIL. Dorian, we can leave whenever you want – don't we have tickets for the theatre? I was looking forward to seeing this Sibyl of yours perform...

HENRY. Shut up, Basil. He's the one – over there – 'He's never seen anyone so marvellous' – that's what he's thinking – go on, I've spent good money – it would be rude not to.

DORIAN. Rude to what?

HENRY. Oh please –

BASIL. – Stop teasing him!

HENRY. Basil, stop being boring –

DORIAN. You are being a bit boring – anyway what would you know?

HENRY. More than you think – at uni Basil was positively –

BASIL. Shut up, Henry – Dorian is far more innocent than we ever were and I intend for it to stay that way –

DORIAN. Too late, Basil – I'm not that innocent –

BASIL. Dorian… are you saying what I think you're saying –

HENRY. Go on, Dorian. Follow him – you know you want to…

BASIL. – Henry.

HENRY. – Basil.

DORIAN. No… *no*… I can't. I won't… It's sibyl. It's Sibyl I want!

HENRY. – Fine, if you won't, I will – don't want a good renter to go to waste. I'll see you at the theatre.

DORIAN. Basil… Come – to the theatre – you shall see Sibyl perform – and see how bright a star she shines – a perfect illusion.

Quick change – the club is now the theatre.

SIBYL. *Oh, what a noble mind is here o'erthrown!*
The courtier's, soldier's, scholar's, eye, tongue, sword,

ONE. Sibyl Vane was certainly lovely to look at…

SIBYL. *Th'expectancy and rose of the fair state,*

TWO. Yet she was curiously listless…

SIBYL. *The glass of fashion and the mould of form,*

ONE. Thoroughly artificial in manner…

SIBYL. *The observed of all observers quite quite down.*

TWO. The voice was exquisite,

ONE. but from the point of view of tone it was absolutely false.

SIBYL. *Blah blah blah blah blah blah blah blah blah blah.*

TWO. The staginess of her acting was unbearable,

ONE. and grew worse as she went on.

TWO. Her gestures became absurdly artificial…

TWO. She spoke the words as though they conveyed no meaning to her…

SIBYL. *Blah blah blah blah blah blah blah blah blah blah.*

ONE. The only person unmoved was the girl herself...

TWO. She is merely, as Henry had said, a commonplace, mediocre, actress.

DORIAN. STOP IT.
STOP THIS.
IT'S SHIT.
IT'S JUST SHIT.

BASIL. Dorian – please – I'm sure she's just ill –

DORIAN. Fuck off, Basil – I must speak to her –

Backstage: SIBYL *looks at him. She is filled with joy.*

SIBYL (*thrilled*). Oh my God! I was so bad tonight!

DORIAN. What was that – what possessed you – what illness, what lack of imagination – my friends were bored. I was embarrassed – the whole thing was pathetic –

SIBYL. I thought you would've understood.

DORIAN. Understood what?

SIBYL. Why I acted so badly. Why I will never act well again –

DORIAN. You mean to say you made yourself ridiculous on purpose? Explain yourself at once.

SIBYL. Don't you get it – I couldn't say those words in that stupid way, the fake lights and the old tights, the brash make-up and the people all staring – I met you and we – you know – and I couldn't pretend any more – you taught me what reality is – it's like in the play – Like a portrait of a sorrow... a face without a heart –

DORIAN. What the fuck are you talking about –

SIBYL. It's *Hamlet*... it's in the play – I... I just meant it was all for you – I couldn't pretend – Don't you understand –

SIBYL *moves closer to* DORIAN, *touches him lightly.*

DORIAN. Don't touch me – You make me sick –

SIBYL. Are you acting? Is this real?

SIBYL *once more attempts to touch* DORIAN, *gently, lovingly.*

DORIAN. I SAID DON'T FUCKING TOUCH ME YOU WORTHLESS PIECE OF CHEAP SHIT.

SIBYL *reels in shock.*

SIBYL. But you said you were going to marry me – kiss me – kiss me again – No, don't turn away from me. My brother warned me about this – no, he was in jest. He didn't mean it. Please – forgive me for tonight? I will work so hard. Try to improve. You're right. Don't leave me. Oh, don't leave me.

DORIAN. This is really quite ugly… I won't see you again. You've disappointed me. Goodbye.

TWO *comes on with a bottle of bleach – they pass it silently to* SIBYL.

TWO. Inquest on an actress: An inquest was held this morning on the body of one Sibyl Vane – an actress recently engaged at the Royal Theatre, Holborn. A verdict of death by misadventure was returned.

THREE. How horribly real ugliness makes things.
Slow curtain, the end.

Applause.

* * *

All turn to the 'painting', which has now changed.

DORIAN. The painting!
Just there.
Can you see it?
It looks… different.
A smirk.
That's right.
Just there.
The face has changed.
Just as I was cruel to the girl.
Trick of the light?
Surely –
Not my face – but the painting's face –

My true nature.
State of me.
I smirked at her.
Some devilry is this –
That whatever I do... I remain the same... beautiful, young,
smooth – and the painting instead will show my sins...
How positively perfect.
Turn the lights off.

THREE. Dorian Gray wakes up – head banging – hungover
with liquor and shame –

TWO. He was cruel to Sibyl Vane.

ONE. Unspeakably so.

TWO. The painting had shown him –

THREE. the error of his ways.

ONE. He would use it to do good.
He would apologise.
Marry the crap actress.
Have affairs and get on with it –
He was composing his apology letter –

TWO. when Henry arrived –

HENRY. Darling Dorian – I have terrible news –

DORIAN. Can't talk, I need to see Sibyl at once –

HENRY. But, dear boy – haven't you seen the papers – Sibyl
Vane... Dead – what a shame... hashtag gone too soon,
hashtag mental health...

DORIAN. What... no! How!
What have I done?

HENRY. Nothing – Sibyl Vane died of her own hand.
'Misadventure.' You should be proud – no girl has ever
downed bleach for me. You inspire acts of great sacrifice,
that is all.

DORIAN. This is awful... I... I was going to make it up to her
– to marry her.

HENRY. Close shave, eh – how lucky you always seem to be –

DORIAN. I should do something – I… I can't bear the idea of my soul being hideous… flowers perhaps? A donation? A celebrity rendition of a Beatles track?

HENRY. How positively good of you, but really you should stop ruining your pretty little face with fretting – come to the opera, it's Balzac – perfectly loud and stompy for us to gossip during the performance. Ooh, I got you a present to cheer you up –

HENRY *passes* DORIAN *a book – the yellow book.*

DORIAN. Another book?

HENRY. This one is special… trust me…

DORIAN. Thank you, Henry… but surely I should… I dunno, buy some sort of mourning – black does suit me…

HENRY. See you at the opera, Dorian – and do stop pretending to be so thoroughly modernly moral… It was simply a lucky escape, that's all – Plus, if one doesn't talk about a thing, it has never really happened.

BASIL *enters, flushed.*

Oh, Basil – what an interesting choice of outfit…

BASIL. Dorian, I came as fast as I could – the news is too terrible. That poor actress – wait, what are you doing?

DORIAN. Getting ready to go out –

BASIL. Dorian – your fiancée has just died –

HENRY. Come along, Dorian – Basil, a lacklustre pleasure as always –

BASIL. Where are you going? To see the poor girl's mother, I hope –

DORIAN. To the opera – didn't you always say art was good for the soul?

BASIL. Dorian, this is horrible! I don't know what has come over you –

DORIAN. Yes it's all very sad but in some ways poetic – an act of great sacrifice, *non*?

BASIL. This callousness – this cruelty –

DORIAN. If one doesn't talk about a thing, it has never really happened.

BASIL. That's one of Henry's – this is all his fault –

DORIAN. I owe a great deal more to Henry than to you – you only ever taught me to be vain.

BASIL. And I'm sure I'll pay for it – but I can't help but want that boy back.

DORIAN. Obviously.
All those days standing around in your studio – mostly undressed with you –
Telling me how pretty I was.
Time of your fucking life.

BASIL. You're right – it was. In fact, it's lovely to see the painting – a reminder of what... could have been – it's strange.

DORIAN. What's strange?!

BASIL. So you have spotted it too –

DORIAN. What?!

BASIL. There's something in that portrait...

DORIAN. Tell me –

BASIL. This is hard for me, Dorian.

DORIAN. Go on!

BASIL. Love... in it.

DORIAN. Ha – I know that, Basil. I thought you meant something else...

BASIL. So my admiration for you – is it that obvious?

DORIAN. In a sad way... yes. It reeks of it.

BASIL. I have always wanted to tell you that – and now I have you can only laugh. It's not what I dreamed of.

DORIAN. Isn't life a bitch – now I really must get to the opera.

BASIL. I don't understand –

DORIAN. Sure you do – you came here to console me – be the shoulder to cry on, and you find me sated, fine – mourned and content – and you can't stand it. You always like to feel superior...

BASIL. That's not... I feel like I've lost you –

DORIAN. I was never yours to own.

BASIL. Goodbye, Dorian – perhaps you're right, perhaps there was never anything more to the painting than your good looks and my ability to paint... it often seems to me that art conceals the artist far more completely than it ever reveals him.

THREE. Remember that, everyone, yeah?

DORIAN. Are you done? There is a whole world out there waiting for me –

Pose.

* * *

Song: 'I Feel Love' by Donna Summer.

THREE. '*A Brave New World.*'

ONE. The Streets of London.

THREE. This isle is full of noises, sweet airs, that delight and hurt not.

TWO. It is a Queer Eldorado.

ONE. Gold, shiny, new hope.

THREE. That time Oscar would visit Kettner's. The Café Royal, Solferino's.

TWO. That time George Paddon went to a ball dressed as Shepherdess of the Golden Age.

ONE. That time I danced to Donna Summer's 'I Feel Love' at Adonis in Tottenham.

TWO. That time we drank each other's sweat at Sink the Pink.

THREE. That time Dorian Gray appeared at a costume ball covered with five hundred and sixty pearls.

ONE. That time I fell in love at The Joiners Arms,

THREE. Princess Diana at the RVT,

TWO. first kiss in Heaven,

ONE. seeing stars at Gutterslut,

THREE. spotted at Dalston Superstore,

TWO. grinding at The Glory,

ONE. the barmaid at The Admiral Duncan,

THREE. the bouncer at Shadow Lounge,

TWO. fighting bears at Comptons,

ONE. sprinting to Chariots,

THREE. Barbies on the ceiling at Friendly Society,

ONE. velvet walls at the Green Carnation –

TWO. Long live the queer spaces.

THREE. That time we marched,

TWO. we sang,

ONE. we danced,

THREE. we shared,

TWO. we cried,

ONE. we laughed until our faces hurt – the vast possibilities of this glorious and colourful city – a present wrapped in glitter and gold – dancing to the beat of our own future – a hard fuck to obliterate our past.

TWO. FOR THE NEXT THIRTY YEARS DORIAN GRAY DID WHATEVER THE FUCK HE WANTED.

ONE. Like what –

THREE. Like everything you could possibly ever think of –

TWO. All because of some book Henry lent him.
    And the freedom the painting gave him –

ONE. A book? – You serious?
    But I thought all art was quite meaningless.

TWO. Well this book was a little bit different… 'indeed, the
    whole book seemed to him to contain the story of his own
    life, written before he had lived it.'

THREE. A bit like *The Picture of Dorian Gray* for Oscar
    Wilde… see what we did there…
    Also it was French. And yellow –

TWO. Follow the Yellow Brick Road!

ONE. It was all about imagination.
    Decadence – aestheticism – camp –

THREE. It was about owning shit.
    For no reason – which Dorian loves.

TWO. And Dorian just buys stuff so much stuff –

DORIAN. Get in, loser, we're going shopping.

THREE. He picks up religions like they're fashion statements.

TWO. Very Madonna Kabbalah noughties chic.

THREE. He starts a cult of his own making – an ode to pure
    hedonism.

    *During the below, the actors bring on a million items from
    all eras. They should be camp, unique, iconic and random.
    One definitely useful item might be a bathtub and a
    candelabra for later. They can stay onstage for the
    remainder of the play.*

DORIAN. I have a collar of pearls, set in four rows. They are
    like unto moons chained with rays of silver. I have amethysts
    of two kinds, one that is black like wine, and the other that is
    red like wine which has been coloured with water. I have
    topazes, yellow as are the eyes of tigers, and topazes that are
    pink as the eyes of wood pigeons, and green topazes that are
    as the eyes of cats –

THREE. Are you finished?

DORIAN. No – I have opals that burn always with an ice-like flame. I have onyxes like the eyes of a dead woman. I have sapphires big like eggs, and blue as blue flowers. I have chrysolites and beryls and chrysoprases and rubies. I have –

THREE. Dorian Gray went round the world,

ONE. jewels and pearls,

TWO. servant girls,

THREE. he fucked men and boys.

TWO. And women.

ONE. Bullied the bastards and drugged-up to his eyeballs.

THREE. He drunk-drove and fought with waiters,

ONE. never mind a few court papers.

TWO. Stormi World and DUIs, Dorian Gray was the world's delight,

ONE. cocaine binges,

TWO. and nights on speed,

THREE. Playboy Mansion and monkey companion.

ONE. Neverland and Jimmy Savile,

TWO. platform heels and Union Jack dresses,

THREE. Elvis Presley feast your heart out,

ONE. Harvey Weinstein's casting couch,

TWO. Ozzy Osbourne ate a bat –

THREE. Marilyn Manson removed some ribs –

ONE. Britney Spears with a pair of shears,

THREE. Lady Gaga's dress of meat,

TWO. Sid and Nancy hotel parties,

THREE. private tigers,

ONE. private plane,

TWO. Gwyneth Paltrow you love to hate,

THREE. (Get that jade egg up your cunt.)

TWO. Courtney Love and Kurt Cobain,

ONE. Paris Hilton's long luscious mane,

TWO. Marilyn Monroe was thirty-six –

THREE. but let's just talk about her tits –

ONE. and then he did it all again...

TWO. And again.

THREE. And again.

ONE. Because nothing is ever enough, and nothing lasts as long as the first time, or takes you there like the last time, and only going further can give you a fraction of what you wanted in the first place.

THREE. Because we all want more –

TWO. And more.

THREE. And more.

TWO. And.

THREE. BEAUTIFUL SINS

ONE. LIKE BEAUTIFUL THINGS

TWO. ARE THE PRIVILEGE OF THE RICH...

TWO. But people started to whisper... the ride was about to get sinister...

ONE. The lights came up – and our gorgeous golden metropolis was filled with shadows of fear, scandal and shame – glitter and gold floating away – never forever – love (for us) is not a permanent thing.

* * *

Lighting change –

OSCAR. How could you, Bosie!

BOSIE. Oh please, Oscar – stop going on and on about it – you ruined a perfect dinner.

OSCAR. But the foolishness of it all, Bosie, I really can't cope with it – my letters – How could you be so flippant with *my* words.

BOSIE. They were in my pocket, they must have fallen out.

OSCAR. And now I have this awful hideous man blackmailing me – asking for all sorts – coming into my hotel rooms, dogging my footsteps.
It's absurd – it's dangerous.

BOSIE. And yet you're the one who refused to pay him! Being mean with your money for absolutely no reason.

OSCAR. I have to cut down – Robbie says.

BOSIE. OH BORING FUCKING WEASELLY MOUTHED LITTLE ROBBIE.

OSCAR. I have to, Bosie, I –

BOSIE. What's the point of all this success if you're not going to enjoy it?

OSCAR. Please understand –

BOSIE. I'm going out – I can't stand this – I can't stand you.

OSCAR. Bosie – no – please –
Please don't say these things to me – it'll all be fine…

BOSIE. Nothing's going to happen – you're Oscar fucking Wilde…

OSCAR. You're right – I'll come.

BOSIE. Good –

TWO. That time in 1885 when an amendment to the Criminal Law Act was added by Liberal MP, Henry Labouchère, to the effect of:

ONE. 'Any male person who, in public, or private, commits, or is party to the commission of, or procures, or attempts to procure the commission by any male person, shall be guilty of a misdemeanour and being convicted thereof shall be liable to be imprisoned for any term not exceeding two years with or without hard labour.'

THREE. Fuck you, Henry Labouchère – Fuck you, Labby.

* * *

ONE. BACK TO ME – BACK TO DORIAN GRAY:

THREE. That time Dorian came home steaming drunk and looked at the portrait.

TWO. The reminder of his new life.

THREE. He has to hide it.

TWO. He hires two heavies to carry it covered into the attic.

THREE. Where he grew up as a boy...

TWO. There's some more to that story probably...

THREE. Locked away in the belly of his youth.

TWO. He puts bolts on the doors,

THREE. chains and more.

TWO. Keeps the keys where only he can find them.

THREE. Knows that, from now on –

DORIAN. What the worm is to the corpse, my sins will be to the painted image on this canvas. They will mar its beauty and eat away its grace. They will defile it – and make it shameful. And yet the thing will live on. It will always be alive –

TWO. And he will be safe –

THREE. perfect – positively youthful.

DORIAN. And that is everything. Pose.

TWO. But some things can't be hidden forever...

OSCAR. Robbie?

ROBBIE. Yes, Oscar, remember me?

OSCAR. Oh please, 'spurned lover' is not a good look on you –

ROBBIE. I haven't time for you to take the piss, Oscar, I must speak with you.

OSCAR. Not now, Robbie, I feel an admonishment coming on and it always gives me a –
Headache.

ROBBIE. You have to stop this – all of this – You're bankrupt.

OSCAR. Am I… Shit… How? My plays are all tremendous successes – did you read the latest review of *Ideal Husband* – they're calling me a genius – *again*.

ROBBIE. Bosie has ruined you – the hotels, the Champagne – the cottages and country houses, the trips to Monte Carlo – the amount you've lost on the tables, pissed up the walls – people are talking – Constance is worried about you – think of your two sons, for what shall they inherit –

OSCAR. My name – and they shall be damn proud of it. And Robbie, my dear, what is this really about – did you want an invitation? Jealousy really is such an ugly emotion –

ROBBIE. Oscar, stop this infatuation with Bosie – please, I beg you – you are terrible for one another. His father, Lord Queensberry –

OSCAR. Don't mention that sadomasochistic pile of sideburns.

ROBBIE. He swears he will ruin you if you are ever seen with his son again, he cannot bear the scandal – it's illegal –

OSCAR. He should really be worrying about the other one who is fucking the Foreign Sec.

ROBBIE. He's dead, Oscar… a shooting… accident.

OSCAR. Accident…

ROBBIE. Exactly, Oscar, I'm being serious – I have a terrible feeling about this –

OSCAR. Drink?

ROBBIE. Listen to me. This is a warning! People are talking –

OSCAR. Good, after all, don't they say – worse than being talked about...

ROBBIE. Goodnight, Oscar –

ROBBIE *exits*.

OSCAR. I wrote a letter to my love,
    And on the way I dropped it,
    One of you have picked it up,
    And put it in your pocket.
    Please, please, drop it, drop it.

* * *

ONE. '*The Victorian Homosexual Quiz – Part Two.*'

TWO. Would you say that sexually you are 'haunted' and 'drawn to one special type of person'?

ONE. Are you given to loving where you do not respect?

TWO. Do such feelings last?

ONE. Has such a person recurrent power over you?

* * *

ONE. On the 18th of February 1895, Lord Queensberry – Bosie's dad – left a card at The Abermarle club, Oscar's club. It read:

TWO. 'For Oscar Wilde, posing sodomite.'

OSCAR. Dearest Robbie,
    Bosies' father has left a card at my club with hideous words on it. I don't see anything now but a criminal prosecution. My whole life seems ruined by this man. If you could come here please do so, I mar your life by trespassing ever on your love and kindness...

    Oscar.

ROBBIE. Don't take the bait. Go to France, Oscar. It's legal there...

ONE. France had decriminalised homosexuality in 1791.

ROBBIE. But whatever you do, please, please don't take him to
court –

ONE. ORDER IN COURT!
A libel case against the Lord Queensbury. For accusing
Oscar Wilde of being a sodomite. Oscar promised his lawyer
that there wasn't… a shred of truth to the claim…
But after three days of court proceedings, Wilde's lawyers
withdrew the lawsuit.
Lord Queensberry was discharged. DISMISSED!

A breath.

* * *

ROBBIE. You lost… Oscar.

OSCAR. Can't talk, Robbie, going to be late for the steamer.

ROBBIE. What – you're leaving – for France? Finally –

OSCAR. For Monte Carlo with Bosie.

ROBBIE. But surely –

BOSIE. – Come on, Oscar, time to go –
Oh, hello, Robbie – interesting choice of outfit.

ROBBIE. Oscar – you need to listen –

BOSIE. Can't waste another moment –
We're going gambling – going to spend it all aren't we,
Oscar?
Try our luck on the cards instead –
Fuck the law.
Off we go – chop chop.

BOSIE *leaves.*

ROBBIE. Oscar, this is madness – you know what his father is
doing right now? Building a case against you – because of
losing to him you've opened the flood gates, they know what
you are now – Oscar – you're going to be arrested –

OSCAR. Let them…

ROBBIE. You don't mean that –

OSCAR. Not a word of it is true… it's all some marvellous fiction.

ROBBIE. Except it isn't.
This isn't one of your plays.

OSCAR. And yet it's about to reach its most startling conclusion – and everyone is oh so ready for the final curtain…

ROBBIE. Pose.

* * *

ONE. BACK TO DORIAN GRAY –

Song: 'Pass That Dutch' by Missy Elliot – the 'Regina George' bit from Mean Girls. *You know the one.*

TWO. Dorian Gray is so hot right now –

THREE. This one time I met Dorian Gray and I got syphilis just by looking at him.

TWO. Did you know that Dorian Gray is a world-famous hand model.

THREE. I heard that Dorian Gray has two tigers – and a huge, huge yacht.

TWO. I saw Dorian Gray wearing pearls and leather chaps; so I bought pearls and leather chaps.

THREE. One time Dorian Gray punched me in the face – it was the best day ever.

DORIAN. IT'S MY BIRTHDAY!

TWO *and* THREE. HAPPY BIRTHDAY!!

DORIAN. Thank you all so so much for coming –
And yes I know I don't look my age.
Funnily enough I've heard that one before…
Another year, another birthday – and yet, look at my face –
Isn't it stunning –
But please do stop asking for the plastic surgeon.
I am – unlike most of you – *au naturel*…
So have another drink – or sniff – Lady Narborough, I see what you're up to.

The scandal –
Now dance, bitchez –
And please do pay me lots of attention.
After all…
IT'S MY FUCKING BIRTHDAY.

*Big blast of pumping party music. Party poppers – a banner
– streamers – balloons.* DORIAN *dances.* BASIL *and*
HENRY *try to join in until they can't really cope…*

BASIL. I'm too old for this.

HENRY. I hate to say it but – we're both too old for this.

BASIL. I told you not to ruin him and look what you did –

HENRY. Oh, come on – he's my greatest achievement.

BASIL. Doesn't even know who he really is –

HENRY. He's a big boy.
Free will – ever heard of it?

BASIL. What I have heard is a dreadful rumour – about what he
did to the Earl of Chester – I was at the club the other day
where everyone was being dreadfully mean about what he's
been up to these past few years –

HENRY. Shhhh, not now, Basil –

BASIL. He's starting to scare me.

HENRY. You're just jealous.

BASIL. Not true.
You realise what's happening here?
He's ruined.
Sullied.
People don't trust him, want to be near him.

HENRY. But look at him.
He's perfect –

BASIL. So why do they say all those awful shocking –

DORIAN. What's that, Basil?

BASIL. I…

HENRY. Dorian, it's been a delightful bash but I'm fucking off
to go fuck someone –
Here, a present.

DORIAN (*unimpressed*). A cigarette case – how funny –

HENRY. To remind you of the day we met – that beautiful day
in Basil's studio –

DORIAN (*cutting him off*). Kisses –

HENRY *leaves, somewhat dejected*. BASIL *and* DORIAN
alone.

Wow, Basil – you're the last man standing – so tell me…
what were you saying about me –

BASIL. Nothing, it's nice to see you – it's been a while… you
never seem to call on me any more.

DORIAN. No I don't… but don't be shy.
You were gossiping, go on…

BASIL. I just… well I just…

DORIAN. Spit it out – after all, don't they say: worse than
being talked about is not being talked about at all –

BASIL. I well I heard something – well the Duke of Berwick –

DORIAN. That old berk – sorry, not funny – do go on.

BASIL. He told me the most shocking story… there was that
boy who committed suicide, he said that you were by his
side – then Lord Henry Ashton – had to leave the country
after one of your… um… parties. Practically hounded, lost
his seat in the Lords – Lord Kent's son – name quite, quite
torn to pieces after that holiday you went on – and Henry's
very own sister – after that evening with you, well – she isn't
allowed to see her own children – I –

DORIAN. And I thought you of all people, Basil – an artist –
would be able to see past the base hypocrisy of our age –
was it my influence that ruined these men – or was I simply
someone who revealed the very beast within – quite literally
with Lord Kent's son –

BASIL. That is not the point, Dorian –

DORIAN. What is then – or do you join those that preach morality so that they can simply slander the next fellow they fancy all over their hideous dinner parties and feel quite, quite smug about themselves –

BASIL. I know our age is not a perfect one – our society baseless, but you should have been a force for good – with your money and your –

DORIAN. *What?* You're getting preachy, Basil.

BASIL. Yes well – maybe it's time you listened to someone else apart from Henry –
And I feel this is my last chance –

DORIAN. Last chance?

BASIL. I'm leaving for Paris tomorrow – and I'm not coming back –

DORIAN. So in a way – this was your leaving party –

BASIL. I suppose… and it was full of beautiful young men – men who will no doubt be dead in six months.

DORIAN. Drama queen –

BASIL. Then tell me – why is your friendship so dangerous to young men?

DORIAN. Dangerous?

BASIL. Yes… I fear you have caused more harm than you know.

DORIAN. Well what you don't know can't really fucking hurt you, can it –

BASIL. Well you just can't – be like that –

DORIAN. Why not?

BASIL. Because… it's horrible and mean and vile and degraded.

DORIAN. Waaah waaah waaah.

BASIL. It's shitty – okay – it's shitty to think that you're just allowed to be a prick. With no consequences. No... fucking punishment –

DORIAN. Wow... you're getting quite cross. If I'm such a terrible human than why can no one can stop looking? Why on earth are they all here drinking my Champagne?

BASIL. Of course they can't stop looking – your face!

DORIAN. What about my face –

BASIL. It's perfect – despite everything they say about you – despite all the years – it's not human –

DORIAN. Do you love me, Basil?

BASIL. I have always loved you –
And you're making fun of me – again – aren't you?

Pause.

I'm just trying to be your friend. But I don't think I really know who you are...

DORIAN. *Oh* Christ, we've done this already, Basil – I'm Dorian Gray.

BASIL. And who is that exactly?

DORIAN. Do you really want to know? Come upstairs with me.

BASIL. Dorian... really... I...

DORIAN. I'm not going to fuck you, Basil – I'm just going to show you something – the real Dorian Gray you seem so keen to meet –

DORIAN *holds out his hand –*

I don't bite...

As DORIAN *moves to 'the attic', he takes a candelabra from onstage – to illuminate the way...*

THREE. He creeps up to the attic.
Unlocks the door.
Dust everywhere.
Mice scuttle into the corners.

And cobwebs cling to his features.
He rips away the curtain.
And there it stands.
The painting.

DORIAN. Ta-dah.

BASIL. Oh Christ!

DORIAN. Don't you love it?

BASIL. What is it??

DORIAN. It's your painting.

BASIL. It can't be – I –

DORIAN. But there's your signature –

BASIL. It's monstrous –

DORIAN. Oh really... but this is me – Basil – the real Dorian
    Gray in all my glory.
    I made a wish all those years ago in your studio – remember?

BASIL. I... no – that's not a thing – it's not human – stop it.

DORIAN. I prayed to swap places with the portrait.

BASIL. It's a trick – the light – it... it's bleeding – leering at me.

DORIAN. Gross, isn't he –

BASIL. – It's evil – you're evil –

DORIAN. This is what your worship gets you –

BASIL. I'm going to pray. Get on your knees with me.

DORIAN. LOL.

BASIL. Stop it, I'm being serious.
    We can solve this – I can save you.
    We will pray.
    STOP LAUGHING PLEASE.
    Our father, who art in heaven, hallowed be my name, thy
    kingdom come... thy... er will be done, I...

DORIAN *lifts* BASIL *onto his feet –* BASIL *stops praying –*

DORIAN. And yet you still want me – Don't you?

DORIAN *kisses* BASIL *– throws him to the floor and smashes the candelabra down on his head – he keeps battering* BASIL *with it over and over – blood spurting – pouring.*

Music builds and builds – huge crescendo.

DORIAN *is covered in blood – blood everywhere – he pants. Fuck –*

THREE. Oscar Wilde was arrested and tried for Homosexuality on the 26th of April 1895.

End of Act One.

Interval.

ACT TWO

We are now in a courtroom.

Even though we are in a courtroom, and the situation is serious, OSCAR *is treating it like a theatre. It's all just another performance. He has a green carnation in his buttonhole.*

Laughter and applause (perhaps use a laughter track, like a sitcom, where the line 'laughter' is indicated).

CARSON. Mr Oscar Fingal O'Flahertie Wills Wilde – those are your names?

OSCAR. Yes.

CARSON. Are you a dramatist and an author?

OSCAR. I believe I am well known as a dramatist – and an author.

Laughter.

CARSON. Will you answer the question simply, please –

OSCAR. Simply – yes...

Laughter.

CARSON. I believe you have taken great interest in matters of art?

OSCAR. Why of course – sorry... yes.

Laughter.

CARSON. And this art that you create – are you concerned as to whether it has a moral or immoral effect?

OSCAR. Not particularly – no –

Laughter.

CARSON. I suggest that so far as your works are concerned you *pose* as not being concerned about morality in particular?

OSCAR. I don't think I understand your meaning of the word 'pose' –

Laughter.

CARSON. 'Pose' is a favourite word of yours, I think –

OSCAR. Is it? – I have no pose in the matter –

Laughter.

...the aim is not to do good or to do evil but to try and make a thing that will have some quality of beauty...

CARSON. 'Beauty'? We shall see – this is one of yours, I think: 'Wickedness is a myth invented by good people to account for the curious attractiveness of others.'
Do you think that is true?

OSCAR. I rarely think that anything I write is true...

Laughter.

Applause – OSCAR *bows* –

A telephone rings. BASIL *is dead in the bath.*

DORIAN. Alan Campbell. It's Dorian – I need a favour.

ALAN. What have you done this time?

DORIAN. Come on over – I'll explain... Quick.

ALAN. Wow – you've brained Basil Hallward... quite the birthday party.

DORIAN. Don't be cute – help me dispose of him –

ALAN. Quickest way to get rid of a body, Dorian – acid. Burns the bones to dust, you can flush it down the toilet... but why on earth should I help you do it –

DORIAN. Because if you don't... I'll tell everyone about... (*Whispers into* ALAN's *ear.*).

ALAN *grows pale. Shakes.*

ALAN. God I hate you.

DORIAN. Yes, well – I'll give you this – (*A baggie of drugs.*) consider it a bonus.

ALAN. I don't do that any more.

DORIAN. That's what they all say –

DORIAN throws the baggie of drugs on the floor. ALAN, despite himself, runs to grab it. DORIAN helps BASIL out of the bath. ALAN grabs a tub of 'bleach' and pours it into the bath (confetti/water/nothing). They all watch 'his body' burn.

Perhaps they smoke...

ALAN exits. The ghost of BASIL goes over to the large frame and lingers there – watching DORIAN speak to his dissolved 'body'.

Oh Basil.
Silly little Basil.
You simply shouldn't have gone sticking your weaselly little nose into other people's business.
What right had you to say those nasty things to me –
You think I'm the bad one – me!
You made me suffer, you sick, perverted, twisted little man.
This is all your fault, anyway –
...Anyway... If you don't talk about something – it never happened...

Song: 'Heart of Glass' by Blondie.

DORIAN sings/performs to this song – gyrating across the stage as the ghost of BASIL creates a Jackson Pollock-esque mess on the 'framed mirror' upstage. They both move and express themselves.

I WANT TO GO DANCING.

(*On the phone.*) Alan. We are going out-out!

POSE. FUCKING POSE.

Techno club music.

ALAN. This place is *it*?

DORIAN. It's called Heaven for a reason.

ALAN. Your posho mates know you come here?

DORIAN. Why shouldn't they –

ALAN. Men on poles – instead of young girls –
How their tongues would wag.

DORIAN. They're already wagging.
Get us a drink then.

ALAN. And to think they used to call you Prince Charming.

DORIAN. Don't you dare call me that – don't you dare ever
utter those words –

ALAN *exits briefly.*

JAMES. Prince Charming!
Oi!
Did he call you – are you – ?

JAMES *lunges and manhandles* DORIAN.

DORIAN. Who the fuck are you – ?

JAMES. James Vane –

DORIAN. Evening, James, now get your cheap hands off me –

JAMES. You killed my sister!

DORIAN. Don't think so, luv.

JAMES. She died for you –

JAMES *grabs hold of* DORIAN *even harder. BDSM vibes
here.*

DORIAN. At least buy me a drink first.

JAMES. My sister, my beautiful sister Sibyl.

DORIAN. Sibyl?… I… I said get off me – darling, this is
suede.

JAMES. I'm going to smash your skull till your brains spill out,
just like I promised her – can you see me, Sibyl –

DORIAN. You're making a mistake – please – listen to me –
I'm not the man you're looking for.

JAMES. Stop fucking talking –

DORIAN. W-when did this young woman die?

JAMES. – Thirty… thirty years ago…

DORIAN. And yet look at my face, dear man, cherubic,
wouldn't you say?
I wasn't born thirty years ago, surely.

JAMES slowly but surely disengages and moves away.

JAMES. She called him Prince Charming –

DORIAN. Nothing but a coincidence…

JAMES. I'm… Sorry… it's just – I thought…
I've lost everything – they're all dead –

DORIAN. So sad.
Do you want to suck me off?

JAMES. I… it'll cost you –

DORIAN. Great… whatever –

JAMES proceeds to suck DORIAN off –

*The ghost of SIBYL is watching on. Now she goes full-on
Ophelia – she chucks green carnations at them and the stage
– very 'That's for remembrance.'*

SIBYL. *O, what a noble mind is here o'erthrown!
The courtier's, scholar's, soldier's, eye, tongue, sword,
Th'expectancy and rose of the fair state,
The glass of fashion and the mould of form,
Th'observ'd of all observers, quite, quite down!
And I, of ladies most deject and wretched,
That sucked the honey of his music vows –*

DORIAN. Go on, say it.

JAMES. Prince Charming…

DORIAN. Good boy.

JAMES. You are him, aren't you?
What the fuck are you?

DORIAN. Nice meeting you –

JAMES. I'll kill you – I will.

DORIAN. I'd get checked out if I were you, I'm riddled…

JAMES. I'll find you – I'll hunt you down –

DORIAN. Toodles – come on, Alan –

DORIAN *exits*. ALAN *pops his head back onstage…*

ALAN. I can tell you where he lives if you like…

JAMES. Why should I trust you?

ALAN. Because I, like everyone else, hate that man's guts –

* * *

TWO. Old Bailey, London. 1895. The Trial of Oscar Wilde.

The laughter and applause become warped…

CARSON. So much for showmanship, Mr Wilde, you are here because you have been accused of no less than twenty-five counts of indecency with other men – twenty-five, of which we will hear details today, and a rather damning amount of evidence –

OSCAR. I can answer to every one.

Warped laughter.

CARSON. We shall see –
Did you ever have any immoral practices with Alfred Wood?

OSCAR. Not guilty.

CARSON. Did you ever open his trousers?

OSCAR. Not guilty.

CARSON. Did you ever put your own person between his legs?

OSCAR. Not guilty.

CARSON. I say to you that several nights in Tite Street you did exactly that.

Warped laughter.

OSCAR. Not guilty.

CARSON. What about Shelley –
    Did you give him whiskey and sodas?

OSCAR. Not guilty.

CARSON. Did you put your hand on his person?

OSCAR. Not guilty.

CARSON. Did you become intimate with a young man named
    James Conway... He was an uneducated lad, wasn't he –

    Warped laughter.

OSCAR. Not guilty.

CARSON. How much money did you give Charles Parker?

OSCAR. Not guilty.

CARSON. You gave him a book, didn't you?

    Warped laughter getting quieter.

OSCAR. Not guilty.

CARSON. Did you take a bedroom for him?

OSCAR. Not guilty –

CARSON. Did you take him for lunch at various places?
    The Café Royal, for example?

OSCAR. Not guilty.

CARSON. Kettner's?

OSCAR. Not guilty.

CARSON. St James's Place?

OSCAR. Not guilty.

CARSON. Solferino's?

OSCAR. Not guilty.

CARSON. What about Fred Atkins – you gave him a cigarette
    case, didn't you – what was that for?

    Warped laughter getting fainter and fainter.

OSCAR. Not guilty.

CARSON. And what about Ernest Scarfe?
Sydney Mavor?
Did they get cigarette cases too?

OSCAR. Not guilty.

CARSON. Wasn't your friend Taylor notorious for introducing
young men to older men?

OSCAR. Not guilty.

CARSON. Did he introduce you to Charles Parker?

OSCAR. Not guilty.

CARSON. And what about Grainger? He alleges you kissed
him –

OSCAR. No – I never kissed him.
He's far too ugly –

CARSON. I find that answer very telling –

OSCAR. No – I –

CARSON. Court adjourned…

Silence.

* * *

TWO. '*The Homosexual Victorian Quiz – Part Three.*'

ONE. Were you petted more than most children?

TWO. Is your wrist flat or round?

ONE. Is there much hair on your body?

TWO. Are your shoulders bony or muscular?

ONE. Do you like to dance, and do you take pleasure in
athletics?

TWO. Would you say that sexually you are 'haunted' and
'drawn to one special type of person'?

ONE. Are you given to loving where you do not respect?

TWO. Do such feelings last?

ONE. Has such a person recurrent power over you?

* * *

OSCAR. Bosie, Bosie, my darling – finally you came –

BOSIE. I can't stay long –

OSCAR. Bosie, it's… it's not going very well and I… I'm worried that maybe… things are going to get worse.

BOSIE. Where's the Champagne – really, this hotel is crumbling at the seams – someone – I'm thirsty.

BOSIE *gets out his cigarette case – takes out a cigarillo.*

OSCAR. Where's the case I gave you –

BOSIE. This is a better one – now, Oscar, I really can't do with you whining all night –

OSCAR. But, Bosie… I'm scared. Your father –

BOSIE. My fucking father! I can't believe he is putting me through this.

OSCAR. He is putting me through this – he started all of this –

BOSIE. For FUCK'S SAKE WHERE IS THE CHAMPAGNE?

OSCAR. Bosie, can't you hear me – I'm scared.

BOSIE. How off-putting – I have an opera to get to –

OSCAR. Bosie! I need you in the court with me – Robbie is there but I need you – why don't you come any more?

BOSIE. I don't know – it stopped being – amusing.

OSCAR. Please come back – to see your gilt soul there would –

BOSIE. Don't get all sentimental, please – your face starts to crease in the most unflattering way –

OSCAR. Bosie… you once said that if I went to jail you would build a house next door – so we could stare at each other through the window – did you mean that –

BOSIE. Look – if you refuse to serve me Champagne I will simply have to go elsewhere –

He goes to leave.

OSCAR. I love you – I will love you always –

BOSIE. Good luck today, Oscar – just remember –If you go down – try not to drag me down with you –

He leaves.

OSCAR *sits there a second, alone… As he leaves,* DORIAN *enters in a birthday hat – he sits alone, listening to opera* (Swan Lake, *perhaps*).

BASIL. Followed by James Vane, Dorian tries to run from his past… most nights he sits locked in the attic – alone – staring at the portrait… He grew more and more enamoured of his own beauty, more and more interested in the corruption of his own soul. He would examine with minute care, and sometimes with a monstrous and terrible delight, the seared lines, the wrinkling forehead… He mocked the misshapen body and failing limbs – wondering sometimes which were the more horrible, the signs of sin, or the signs of age.

T*he ghost of* SIBYL *is creating mayhem in the space, like a kid at a party…*

SIBYL. He's coming, you know. My big brother's gonna get you –

DORIAN. Come on, be nice, Sibyl. My nerves are shredded – won't you speak some Shakespeare to me – do your Juliet… you know you were very good –

SIBYL. Nahhhh I don't do that shit any more – I've moved on. It's so much better when no one gets to tell you what to do…

DORIAN. Stop making a mess – this place is a muck heap – Anyway, it's my fucking birthday! Where is everyone??

SIBYL *has fun smearing stuff over the portrait.*

SIBYL (*sing-song*). Ha, no one's come to your paaaarty – nobody likes you, everybody hates you – they all say –

DORIAN. Basil? Are you there? Come and tell me what you think of your portrait now –

SIBYL. Basil doesn't like to play –

DORIAN. God, look at it – it is hideous.

SIBYL. It's fucking revolting. Look, you can still see my smirk. Rightttt… there.

A noise.

DORIAN. What was that?

SIBYL. I told you he was coming – James, can you see meeeee?

DORIAN. James?!
    Where is he – ?

SIBYL. Any minute now…

DORIAN. Is he there?
    Hello?

SIBYL. You okay, babes?

DORIAN. Who's that?
    That – there.
    Lock the doors.
    Fuck it, I don't feel safe alone any more – I must not be alone.

SIBYL. HE'S BEHIND YOU. You better run!

DORIAN. Fuck!

SIBYL. This is fun.

    DORIAN *picks up the phone.*

DORIAN. Hello. Bring the Bentley round. I need to leave. I don't know – the country estate.

He slams the phone down and leaves.

JAMES *enters.*

SIBYL. He went that way!

JAMES. DORIAN GRAY I'M GOING TO BREAK YOUR NECK –

Song: 'Country House' by Blur.

A very big house in the country. DORIAN *and* HENRY *enter in hunting garb – Chelsea mum by way of* Ab Fab. *To avoid the need for stage guns, perhaps use old-fashioned umbrellas from the set.*

HENRY. What-ho – Dorian, noicceee party here in your country manor estate mansion thing – I'm like faaaaack, so out of breath, can you just. One second.

DORIAN. I thought you said you could hunt, Henry.

HENRY. Used to, old boy, used to.

DORIAN. I'm not an old boy, babe – but you are.

HENRY. And I feel it… sometimes bits of my face fall off into my hands… thank God for Botox.

DORIAN. I can't relate.

HENRY. No… you're still just as glorious as they day we met – my little boy-woy.

DORIAN. Radiant you called me.

HENRY. Hmmm… that day in Basil's stuffy old studio –
In fact, have you heard from him – they say no one has seen him for months – most mysterious – probably the most interesting thing he's ever done, disappear.

DORIAN. I know nothing about it –

HENRY. It has to be said he was getting pretty shit with age – his art had gone right off.
– Something so embarrassing about someone still daring to be creative after thirty… If only we could all be like you, Dorian – positively youthful…

DORIAN. Jealousy is such an ugly emotion, Henry.

HENRY. And yet you fancy it the most.

DORIAN. Pity it, more like –

HENRY. Touché. Haven't I taught you well?
Oh yes – did you read about that Alan chap in the newspaper this morning – reading between the lines he overdosed – you knew him, didn't you?

DORIAN. Years ago… he never could say no – What was that?!

HENRY. What?
I didn't hear anything – my hearing aids – one sec –

DORIAN. Over there.

HENRY. Well get your gun out – probs a pheasant or a hare –

DORIAN. There.

HENRY. Where?

DORIAN. James!

HENRY. Who the fack is that –

JAMES. Found you –

JAMES *and* DORIAN *point their guns at one other*.

HENRY. Well this is exciting…

JAMES. Prince fucking Charming – you took everything from me –

DORIAN. How did you find me?

JAMES. So many people hate you –

DORIAN. And yet I'm constantly surrounded by them.

HENRY. Blow the pauper's brains out –

JAMES. I'm going to finally make you pay for everything – for Sibyl.

DORIAN. And who's she again –

JAMES. You're the devil –

DORIAN. Go on, James… shoot…

JAMES. This is for my si–

DORIAN *has already shot him*.

Pause. DORIAN *realises what he's done – that he's free – he's won again… just… But something has shifted…*

HENRY. Sentiment always drags a man down.

DORIAN. It's over… I won… he's gone!

HENRY. Are you crying?

DORIAN. Tell everyone the party is over. I'm bored of the countryside –

HENRY. Something has changed, hasn't it?

DORIAN. Yes, I'm free now… finally fucking *free*!

DORIAN *is elated. Free at last. Dancing, relief – but this is short-lived –*

* * *

THREE. '*The Anatomy of Lying – Part Two.*'

TWO. There are several reasons why people tell lies:

THREE. To protect themselves from punishment or embarrassment,

TWO. to protect their own fantasies about themselves,

THREE. to protect the feelings – or, in extreme cases, the lives – of others.

TWO. The lies Dorian has told:

THREE. 'I'm going for a walk.'

TWO. 'I'll be away for the weekend.'

THREE. 'I went out with a friend.'

TWO. 'I didn't kill Basil.'

THREE. 'I've got a headache.'

TWO. 'I didn't kill Sibyl.'

THREE. 'I was drunk.'

TWO. 'Alan Who?'

THREE. 'I don't care about the portrait.'

TWO. The truth is rarely pure –

THREE. and never simple.

* * *

Darkness descends. DORIAN *stares at the portrait.*

DORIAN. I'm free
   finally fucking free
   no one can touch me –
   The only thing left is you –
   You are more hideous, more gruesome than ever.
   Every single second you atrophy crumble rot.
   And I stay the same.
   Beautiful perfect.
   Taunting.
   God I hate you – but it's over – it's over now –

BASIL. It will never be over, Dorian.

DORIAN. Basil?

SIBYL. Poor stupid man – He still doesn't get it.

BASIL. Look at the painting – really look at it – my best work –

SIBYL. Excrement and tears, shit and bile –

BASIL. It will never be over.

SIBYL. You silly little boy-woy.

BASIL. Not with that hideous thing looking and leering.

SIBYL. Judging.

BASIL. Proving who you really are –

The ghosts laugh at him, vicious and maniacal.

DORIAN. That's not who I am…
   I… I'm going to change.
   I am.
   STOP LAUGHING.
   I'll prove you all wrong –

SO WHY DON'T YOU JUST FUCK OFF – JUST FUCK
OFF –
I'm going to be free!

DORIAN *exits*.

BASIL. And so he left…

SIBYL. And no one knew where he'd gone…

BASIL. House boarded up.

SIBYL. Shut up.

BASIL. Locked up.

SIBYL. Trespassers will be prosecuted…
Bless.

* * *

TWO. Old Bailey. London. 1895. The Trial of Oscar Wilde.

CARSON. Today we have heard you deny your corruption of a
stream of ill-educated young men, but I would suggest to the
court that everything about this corruption is contained in
your novel – *The Picture of Dorian Gray* – a story of a
young man who sells his soul in order to carry out acts of
gross indecency – where a sort of 'magical painting' of him
becomes hideous and he remains beautiful.

OSCAR. It's a little more nuanced than –

CARSON. I would say that this book – this work of art as you
call it – is not a novel but a handbook that promotes vice,
sodomy and worse –

OSCAR. It is a *book*, sir – it cannot convince anyone to do
anything – there is no such thing as a bad influence – you
must remember that novels and life are different things –

CARSON *holds up the book*.

CARSON. We shall see – now listen to the part where the artist
in the book confesses hin love to Dorian Gray, I believe it
was left out of the purged edition afterwards.

OSCAR. I deny the expression 'purged'.

CARSON. You don't call it 'purged' but we will see... page fifty-six, my lord... I shall read it out for the good of the court room:
'Dorian... It is quite true that I have worshipped you with far more romance of feeling than a man usually gives to a friend. Somehow, I have never loved a woman... I quite admit that from the moment I met you, your personality had the most extraordinary influence over me... I adored you madly, extravagantly, absurdly...'

Have you yourself ever had that feeling towards a young man, Mr Wilde?

OSCAR (*played for a laugh*). I have never given adoration to anybody but myself –

Silence.

CARSON. And yet this book – this work of art of yours – is full of sordid adoration for men, vice, sodomy – and it doesn't seem to have stayed on the page, Mr Wilde – it seems to have been but a mirror for your own life –

OSCAR. No – that's not true –

CARSON. I would suggest that you are guilty of every single charge that has been brought against you – in fact, I would suggest that you, sir, are a *liar*.

OSCAR. No –

ONE. Oscar Wilde was convicted of gross indecency and received two years of hard labour in Reading Gaol.

OSCAR. My God, my God. And I? May I say nothing, my lord?

ONE. That time six hundred gentlemen crossed the channel on the night of Oscar's conviction.

TWO. That time George Paddon was arrested in drag, put on trial and laughed at in court.

ONE. That time George Michael was arrested and forced to come out.

THREE. That time Oscar's house in Tite Street was cleared out and everything in it was auctioned off.

TWO. That time The Admiral Duncan…

ONE. Green Carnation died, the Joiners empty, Chariots gone.

TWO. That time Oscar's name was taken off the theatres in which two of his plays were currently showing.

THREE. That time his shows were cancelled.

TWO. That time I was spat at on the street.

THREE. That time Oscar was spat at in Clapham Junction on his way to Reading.

ONE. That time –

OSCAR. Dear Bosie,
After long and fruitless waiting I have determined to write to you myself, as much for your sake as for mine, as I would not like to think that I had passed through two long years of imprisonment without ever having received a single line from you, or any news or message even, except such as gave me pain…

ONE. On May the 19th 1897, Oscar Wilde left Reading Gaol, ostracised from society – he boarded a ship for France immediately.

* * *

OSCAR. Robbie! You came.

ROBBIE. Oscar –

OSCAR. Sebastian Melmoth actually –

ROBBIE. Of course – I forgot…

OSCAR. Sadly I never do…
It is the only lie I still allow myself.
I have learnt – the hard way – the beauty of truth.

He coughs/splutters.

ROBBIE. What did the doctor say?

OSCAR. Not long now – Drink?

ROBBIE. Is it wise –

OSCAR. Death doesn't want me sober – no one ever did.

ROBBIE. I did…

OSCAR. Hmm, you've been good to me, Robbie.

ROBBIE. And yet…
   I'm not Bosie.

OSCAR. How is he?

ROBBIE. Why do you still care?

OSCAR. I can't help it… does he know – that I'm ill –

ROBBIE. Possibly.

OSCAR. Will you tell him?
   That I –

ROBBIE. Yes, as much as it pains me…
   He never did deserve you.
   No one did.

OSCAR. You gave it your best.

ROBBIE. Rest…

OSCAR. I can't –

   He coughs/splutters.

ROBBIE. I'm working on getting all your works back.
   Making sure the fakes are rounded up and disposed of –
   I'm going to make sure they're known, Oscar…
   Forever.
   Can you imagine?
   You'll be one of the greats –
   Lauded by the very country and society that rejected you –
   that locked you away.
   They will be saying your name at dinner parties again – as if
   they deserved to…
   Oscar?…

OSCAR. Society, as we have constituted it, will have no place
   for me, has none to offer; but *Nature*, whose sweet rains fall
   on unjust and just alike, will have clefts in the rocks where
   I may hide, and secret valleys in whose silence I may weep

undisturbed. She will hang the night with stars so that I may walk abroad in the darkness without stumbling, and send the wind over my footprints so that none may track me to my hurt: she will cleanse me in great waters, and with bitter herbs make me whole.

OSCAR *sings 'Lush Life' by Billy Strayhorn.*

* * *

DORIAN *enters during the song and sits alone onstage, drinking.*

The phone rings. DORIAN *answers.*

DORIAN. Yes, I'll come –

The hospital.

You called me – I've come to say goodbye to Woots... sorry, I mean, Henry Wotton...

NURSE. He's in his room, just down this corridor.

DORIAN. It smells of old people... and eggs...

NURSE. It's an old person's home so yeah... that's about right.

DORIAN. Sorry I don't really do old...

NURSE. He's just had his medication so he might be a bit wobbly – go easy – he hasn't got long...

DORIAN. You remind me of someone.

NURSE. I've never met you – I would remember someone like you.

DORIAN. Why – because I'm beautiful? I'm sorry, I don't know why I said that –

NURSE. Henry – look – you have a visitor...

HENRY. Dorian – you came back, I knew you would.

DORIAN. Henry – you're... you look... like / death...

HENRY. So beautiful – radiant... your skin...

DORIAN. There's something I need to tell you –

HENRY. Do you remember it – the day we met?
The studio was filled with the rich odour of roses –

DORIAN. Yes, Henry – I need you to listen to me now –

HENRY. Now to realise oneself completely – that is the aim of
the age.

DORIAN. Henry –

HENRY. You know that when you age – all this will be taken
from you – time is a jealous bitch and she will savage a face
like yours, / so use it, child – use it whilst you can –

DORIAN. You've told me this – you've said this –

HENRY. Our limbs fail, our senses rot, we crumble into hideous
puppets, / we atrophy until we die.

DORIAN. I *know* this, Henry, it's why I made that stupid
fucking wish, it's why you made me do this to myself –

HENRY. I didn't make you do anything – you stupid little boy –

DORIAN. So you *can* hear me... and that's not true, Henry – I
was better once I remember it – until you poisoned me with a
book. I should not forgive that, Henry, you ruined my life –
It could have been different – you must promise to never to
give that book to anyone –

HENRY. Poisoned by a book!... There is no such thing as that.
Art has no influence upon action. My dear boy, you really
are beginning to moralise... you sound like sad old Basil –

DORIAN. Basil – that's why I've come here –
I... I... There was an accident, an incident, Basil, at my
birthday party all those years ago... he provoked me really, a
misunderstanding but I... I hit him and...
Well I killed him –
I killed Basil...

HENRY. Did you?... But he's over there –

BASIL *waves*.

Now where did you go for all those years? We've missed
you...

Pause. DORIAN sees that HENRY truly does not care about him being a murderer. The ghost of BASIL has simply joined in – it is a nightmare and horribly reminiscent of the first scene.

DORIAN. I… I went to a yoga retreat in India, amazing place, really very spiritual. I've changed, Henry, truly. I know what it is to abstain… I'm doing a twelve-step programme and I wanted you to know about Basil before you… so you can forgive me and tell me it's all alright –

HENRY *and the ghost of* BASIL *laugh at him.*

HENRY. You can't change, Dorian, that's the point. You can say all the Hare Krishnas you want, we all know what you're truly capable of. The rebrand fools no one, you fucking idiot.

DORIAN. I have changed. I swear it. I am good now. I give to charity, I help old ladies with their shopping. STOP LAUGHING!

HENRY. It reminds me of *Hamlet* – do you remember we saw it – Sibyl, that was her name – she played Ophelia… and she was rubbish. There's a quote, isn't there…

'Like the painting of a sorrow,
A face without a heart…'

It's you. You have never changed. Pure vanity. Fabulously so.

DORIAN.…I don't want to hear this. You're senile and deranged – I've changed.

BASIL *and* HENRY *laugh.*

HENRY. Oh please… whatever this is, this hideous mask – it is of your own making – I think I see a wrinkle.

He smiles at DORIAN. DORIAN *abruptly grabs a pillow and smothers* HENRY *to death. Feathers everywhere.*

HENRY *is now dead. The struggle over. The ghost of* BASIL/NURSE *wheel* HENRY *away.* DORIAN *alone.*

DORIAN. Oh shit, I shouldn't have done that.
Henry – forgive me.
Please.

It was just an accident.

One last slip-up.

I won't let it happen again.

Promise.

Because I'm going to be good from now on.

I worked so hard these last few years.

I really did try.

It was only a moment – it doesn't count.

That's not who I am any more and I –

Shut up – all of you, shut up.

I can hear you laughing still.

No, I'm good and worthy and well-behaved.

I help old ladies with their shopping.

I give to charity.

I'm wholesome and good.

So good.

I don't misbehave.

I shall look at the painting – and that will prove my good intentions.

There.

It's...

It's...

Still as fucked-up and hideous.

No –

I refuse.

The spell is clearly broken.

Something is wrong with it –

I shall destroy it.

Of course.

I shall kill it and be set free finally.

To be good.

So good.

I'm going to be good and clean.

And free.

He goes and grabs the candelabra – makes to strike the portrait.

I will kill you – once and for all –

OSCAR *appears onstage.*

OSCAR. My poor boy, my poor Dorian. Drink?

DORIAN. Excuse me. I'm kind of in the middle of something here.

OSCAR. Do you mind if I watch?

DORIAN. With pleasure.

> DORIAN *makes to continue. He raises the candelabra.*

I WILL BE FR–

OSCAR (*interrupting*). *The Picture of Dorian Gray* by Oscar Wilde. It really is my best work. Don't you think?

DORIAN. No. It is a lie.

OSCAR. True. But I am a born liar. We both are.

DORIAN. How far did you go?

OSCAR. As far as I possibly could.

DORIAN. Yeah, me too.

OSCAR. It is such a shame we had to lie, don't you think? What a life it must be to be free of that necessity. Can you imagine it? A world where we don't have to hide a version of ourselves in the attic of our childhood. What a queer thing. It really doesn't turn out well for anyone in the end.

> OSCAR *looks at the painting.*

It is a hideous monstrosity. Mawkish and nauseous.

DORIAN. Unclean. Contaminating. I hate it.

OSCAR. Why must I go grubbing in muck heaps?

DORIAN. So sad.

OSCAR. It really is a hideous work of art.

DORIAN. All art is quite useless.

OSCAR. Correct.

DORIAN. All life is quite useless.

OSCAR. No, my poor boy. How young you are. Human life is the one thing worth investigating. Compared to it there is nothing else of any value. To live is the rarest thing in the world. Most people exist, that is all.

DORIAN. But I live only a life of regret.

OSCAR. To regret one's own experiences is to arrest one's own development. To deny one's own experiences is to put a lie into the lips of one's own life. It is no less that the denial of the soul.

DORIAN. Ah, but I don't have one of those.

OSCAR. Therein lies the rub.

DORIAN. Ugh, I wish I could have loved – but I was forever too focused on myself.

OSCAR. I know. It's a habit of mine too –

DORIAN. I went mad in search for new sensations. I sprinted towards them, endlessly. I hurt everyone. All because I couldn't love –

OSCAR. I know. But loving isn't easy for us, my boy –

They hold hands, a moment – OSCAR *quickly breaks contact.*

I better let you get on.

OSCAR *leaves the frame.*

DORIAN (*calling after him, softly*). Thank you.

Perhaps OSCAR *looks back.*

TWO. Dorian creeps up to the attic.

DORIAN *exits.*

Unlocks the door. Dust everywhere. Mice scuttle into the corners. Cobwebs cling to his features. And there it stands. The picture itself – that was evidence. He would destroy it. Once it had given him pleasure to watch it changing and growing old. The thrill of the secret. The thrill of the double life. The lie. But, of late he had felt no such pleasure. He would destroy it. He looked around – and saw the knife that had stabbed Basil Hallward. This would kill the past, and when it was dead then he would be free. He seized the thing, and stabbed the picture with it...

ONE *and* THREE *re-enter.*

THREE. Oscar Wilde died in a hotel room in Paris 1900 – the dawn of a new century. Forty-six years old.

TWO. In 1967 the law that sent Wilde to prison was abolished.

THREE. Fifty years later Wilde was among an estimated fifty thousand men who were pardoned for homosexual acts that were no longer considered offences under the Policing and Crimes Act 2017.

ONE. We have been posing as three Victorian gentlemen –

THREE. Henry,

TWO. Basil,

ONE. and Dorian.

THREE. We have been posing as three Victorian sodomites –

TWO. Robbie,

ONE. Bosie,

THREE. and Oscar.

ONE. *All art is at once surface and symbol.*

TWO. *Those who read beneath the surface do so at their peril.*

THREE. *It is the spectator, and not life, that art really mirrors.*

ONE. *Diversity of opinion about a work of art shows that the work is –*

THREE. *new –*

ONE. *complex –*

TWO. *and vital.*

ONE. *When critics disagree –*

THREE. *the artist is in accord with himself.*

ONE. *We can forgive a man for making a useful thing as long as he does not admire it.*

THREE. *The only excuse for making a useless thing –*

TWO. *is that one admires it intensely.*

THREE. Oscar fucking Wilde.

TWO. The truth is rarely pure –

THREE. and never simple.

ONE. Pose.

> *Green carnations explode from the ceiling, petals and shine.*

> *End.*

Polari

Polari is a collection of words used as a secret informal language. It was particularly popular with gay men between the 1920s and 1960s, in order to avoid imprisonment while homosexuality was illegal in England and Wales.

However, Polari had sprung up in the 1700s and 1800s as a secret language of relatively powerless groups considered to be on 'on the wrong side of the law'. This included travelling performers, sailors and Roma people – and many of its words, in fact, derive from the Romany people scattered across Europe. The *Oxford English Dictionary* says it is 'made up of Italianate phrases, rhyming slang and cant terms'.

In the play we use Polari when Henry is introducing Dorian to the 'beautiful London' – the Queer Eldorado. At first Dorian doesn't speak the language, but by the end of the section he has started to pick it up and understand.

Glossary

Ajax   Next to

Bona   Good/beautiful

Bona to vada your dolly old eek!   Good to see your nice face.

Cartso   Penis

Drag   Clothing (usually the sort you're not expected to wear)

Ecaf   Face (back-slang), can be shortened to 'eek'

Fantabulosa   Wonderful

Lallies   Legs

Martinis   Hands

Naff   Rubbish (urban legend has it that 'naff' is an acronym for 'not available for fucking')

Omi/omee   Man

Omi palone   A gay/effeminate man

Trade   Sex/casual sexual partner

Vada   To look

Vada the naff strides on the omi ajax   Look at the awful trousers on the man nearby.

Zhoosh, zhuzh   To style/to do up (give your hair a quick zhoosh)

Other Resources

Putting on the Dish

A short film made in 2015, features Polari in action. It's free to view and focuses on a conversation between two men in Polari.

Polari: The code language gay men used to survive

bbc.com/culture/article/20180212-polari-the-code-language-gay-men-used-to-survive

Fabulosa! The Story of Polari, Britain's Secret Gay Language

Professor Paul Baker at the University of Lancaster has written several books and articles on the subject.
wp.lancs.ac.uk/fabulosa/whats-polari

A Queer Code: Polari, the secret language you need to know

blog.yorksj.ac.uk/englishlit/a-queer-code-polari-the-secret-language-you-need-to-know

Suggested Bibliography

The Real Trial of Oscar Wilde by Merlin Holland

Queer City by Peter Ackroyd

Oscar: A Life by Mathew Sturgis

Who Was That Man?: A Present for Mr Oscar Wilde by Neil Bartlett

Only Dull People Are Brilliant at Breakfast by Oscar Wilde

London and the Culture of Homosexuality 1885–1914 by Matt Cook

A Queer Little History of Art by Alex Pilcher

Oscar Wilde and His Circle by Simon Callow

A Nick Hern Book

DORIAN first published in Great Britain in 2021 as a paperback original by Nick Hern Books Limited, The Glasshouse, 49a Goldhawk Road, London W12 8QP, in association with Reading Rep Theatre

Cover image: Muse Creative Communications

Designed and typeset by Nick Hern Books, London
Printed in the UK by Mimeo Ltd, Huntingdon, Cambridgeshire PE29 6XX

A CIP catalogue record for this book is available from the British Library

ISBN 978 1 83904 051 1

www.nickhernbooks.co.uk

facebook.com/nickhernbooks

twitter.com/nickhernbooks